ENGLISH
LANDSCAPES

ROB TALBOT AND ROBIN WHITEMAN

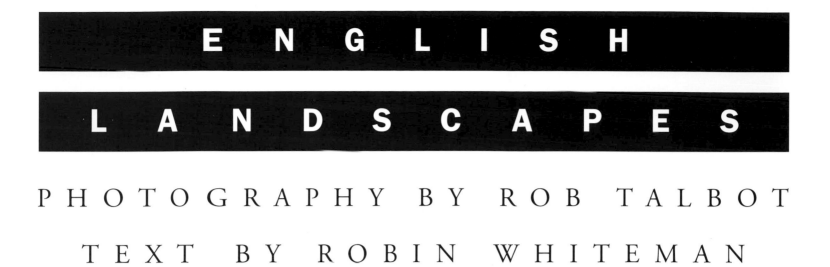

ENGLISH LANDSCAPES

PHOTOGRAPHY BY ROB TALBOT

TEXT BY ROBIN WHITEMAN

GREENWICH
EDITIONS

Text and Photographs
© Talbot-Whiteman, 1995

The right of Rob Talbot and Robin
Whiteman to be identified as the Authors
of this Work has been asserted by them in
accordance with the Copyright, Designs &
Patents Act, 1988

First published in 1995 by
George Weidenfeld & Nicolson Ltd

Paperback edition first published in 1997 by
Phoenix Illustrated

This edition published in 2004 by Greenwich
Editions, The Chrysalis Building, Bramley Road,
London W10 6SP
An imprint of **Chrysalis** Books Group plc

British Library Cataloguing-in-Publication Data
A catalogue record for this book is available from
the British Library

ISBN 0-86288-611-2

Edited by Laura Washburn
Designed by Harry Green
Litho origination by Newsele Litho Spa
Printed and bound in Italy

Half-title page: Stock Beck, Ambleside, Cumbria

Title page: Oare, Exmoor, Somerset

ACKNOWLEDGEMENTS
Robin Whiteman and Rob Talbot would
particularly like to acknowledge the
generous co-operation that English
Heritage and the National Trust have
extended to them over the last ten years
(which includes all the Regional Offices, as
well as both Head Offices). Particular
thanks go to Diana Lanham, Manager of
the National Trust Photographic Library,
and Barbara Morley, former Regional
Public Affairs Manager, the National Trust
Severn and Mercia Regions. They are also
extremely grateful to the following:
Christopher Zeuner, Director, Weald and
Downland Open Air Museum; John
Manley, Chief Executive, the Sussex
Archaeological Society; the Hon. Simon
Howard and Castle Howard Estate Ltd; the
Curators of the Sheldonian Theatre,
Oxford; the Director, Furzey Gardens,
Minstead; Philip Jackson, Manager, Minack
Theatre. Our appreciation also extends to
all those individuals and organizations too
numerous to mention by name who
nevertheless have made such a valuable
contribution to this and all our previous
books. Special thanks go to Colin Grant,
our editor on most of the 'Country Series':
and last, but by no means least, Michael
Dover and Ted Smart for making this book
possible, and Laura Washburn for all her
support as its editor.

CONTENTS

INTRODUCTION

Fisher Crag Plantation,
Thirlmere, Cumbria

It was not until the Spring of 1971, when I returned to the UK after a six-month filming expedition in North Africa and the Sahara, that I fully appreciated the richness, beauty and infinite variety of the English countryside. Starved of greens – saturated, instead, with reds, yellows, ochres and browns – I arrived on English soil to find almost every patch of unbuilt land ablaze with a spectrum of shimmering and vibrating colour. It wasn't simply the blossoming flowers that scintillated and danced before my unaccustomed eyes, but every shade of green imaginable. As my eyes gradually grew accustomed to the colours, so their vividness faded and became far less overwhelming. Happily, however, I was left with a deep reverence for the English landscape that, ten years later, manifested itself in a trilogy of films celebrating William Shakespeare, Stratford-upon-Avon and the Warwickshire countryside. As it happened, the success of these films not only introduced me to the world of publishing, it also introduced me to Rob Talbot.

Ours, on reflection, seemed an unlikely partnership; Rob was a freelance sports photographer, and I was a documentary producer/director, who had written for films. When we first met in the early 1980s, each pursuing quite separate careers, neither of us could have foreseen that in 1995 we would both be 'authors', celebrating ten years of a working partnership that had produced some fifteen books on the English countryside, almost half a million published words, and countless thousands of colour photographs.

Despite the fact that Rob took all the pictures for our first book, *Shakespeare Country*, it was not until *The Cotswolds* that the partnership of writer and photographer officially began. In those heady days, to save costs, much of the time we travelled to locations together, sharing vehicles and walking wherever possible. As well as gathering my own research, I acted as Rob's photographic assistant, doing everything from helping carry the equipment to persuading a determined 'star character' to move out of shot. For, even then, it was Rob's policy to try and exclude people, cars, unsightly telegraph wires and other extraneous clutter. Great effort was also made to clear the scene of rubbish, even if it meant one of us picking up a broom to sweep the pavements clean or wading knee-deep into a stream to pluck a conspicuous plastic bottle out of the weeds.

But, despite all the care, planning and meticulous attention to detail that went into each and every shot, the weather proved frustratingly unpredictable. On one memorable occasion, in the winter of 1986, while we were on Fish Hill above Broadway in the Cotswolds, a freak and sudden blizzard turned the landscape white, the

sheep to hummocks and the roads to glass. It was so cold that when Rob tried to take a photograph the molecules in one of his filters somehow underwent a fundamental change, rendering it useless. By the time we eventually returned to our respective homes in the Midlands, not without incident, we learned that the sudden snowfall had caused such havoc in the Cotswolds, cutting off countless villages, that it warranted inclusion in the national television news.

Talbot's weather-Jonah, which was to dog him ever after, had made its presence felt with quite dramatic consequences.

South Front, Castle Howard, near Malton, North

Our next book, *The English Lakes*, proved to be more of a challenge than anticipated. Despite the proximity of 'Shakespeare Country' and the Cotswolds to our homes in the Midlands, we had both managed to clock up surprisingly high mileage. Rob's vehicle had been virtually driven into the ground, while mine had devoured so much petrol that it had to be exchanged for one that was far more economical.

The Lake District was much further away. More often than not, instead of making day trips when the weather turned favourable, Rob had to stay away for extended periods. The popularity of the region, however, with the tourist season lasting for twelve months of the year, made it difficult to find accommodation at a moment's notice. Hotels were ruled out as being too expensive. Camping seemed the cheapest and most obvious solution.

That was before Rob's weather-Jonah decided to empty the heavens on the fells, and, in consequence, flood the campsite he just happened to be sleeping in.

Bed and Breakfast accommodation brought further problems. As Rob needed to be up and at his pre-planned location by the crack of dawn, so he required bed, but no breakfast which was not always well received.

To complicate matters further, on his first foray into the spectacular landscape of the English Lakes he found that his traditional working methods proved inadequate and he left after taking only a couple of pictures.

Charlecote Park and the River Avon, Warwickshire

Having found a promising scene, he set the camera up on its tripod and began looking through the viewfinder to fine tune the composition. By moving the camera slightly to the right, he discovered that the shot improved. A little further to the right and it was even better. Just a fraction more...

It was then that he became aware of the fact that he had panned the camera virtually a full 360 degrees and was back with almost the original scene!

On reflection, he realised that he had reacted *emotionally* to the landscape, and had not stopped to consider which specific aspects of the scene could best be captured on film. With so many stunning pictorial possibilities concentrated within a relatively small area, the latter approach was absolutely essential.

From that moment on, Rob worked slowly and methodically, visiting potential locations many times, taking compass readings, making notes, marking the best positions for the camera, anticipating what kind of light or mood would do the scene justice, and generally doing as much groundwork as possible to get the maximum out of each day. With clear and carefully thought-out objectives, when (and if) all the elements came together, taking the actual photographs was relatively easy.

I had other priorities. Not least, in trying to keep up with the youthful Rob, who thought nothing of clambering to the top of the fells by the steepest and quickest means possible; or standing for hours in the shallows of a freezing lake, waiting for the light to be just right; or sacrificing lunch in order to get as much done as was feasible during daylight hours. His feats of physical endurance were to become almost legendary.

Danby Head, Danby Dale, North Yorkshire

A 'Landscape Masterclass' article on him in *Photo Answers* magazine prompted a reader from Harrow to write in and enquire about the state of his health and fitness. Apparently, the reader's medium-format outfit weighed in at just under 30lbs.

'On a long hot day,' he wrote, 'I managed around fifteen miles, stopping frequently to rest and take pictures. Needless to say, by the evening I was completely knackered, and this was over fairly easy terrain. Rob Talbot's kit must exceed 40lbs and, judging by the photographs, he goes to some pretty remote locations. Assuming they're as inaccessible as they look, how does he get all his equipment there? Does he employ an assistant, pack-horse, motorized trolley? If not, could you publish details of Rob's diet and fitness regime so that us lesser mortals can at least gain an insight into how this physical superman manages such feats of strength and endurance?'

Owlpen, Gloucestershire

Despite Rob's insistence that he carried only *selected* items of equipment, *never* all of it at once, the editor stubbornly maintained that he had last been seen flying past the office window in a red and blue suit!

Not only did I have to try to match Rob's superhuman feats, I had to stay awake long enough to do my own research. In order to take advantage of a break in the weather, which was frequently abysmal, I found myself making what came to be called 'the dash'. Getting up early in the morning, arriving just before dawn, spending the entire day dashing from one location to another, then returning home to the Midlands, usually in the early hours of the following morning.

In contrast to the quiet launch of *Shakespeare Country* in the Spring of 1987, the publication of *The Cotswolds* in the autumn found Rob and I, if only fleetingly, the centre of media attention.

On one embarrassing occasion we found ourselves at a country show, inside the tent of BBC Radio Oxford, waiting to be interviewed. Rob, who had a bit of broadcasting experience, was so relaxed that the interviewer, thinking that he had fallen asleep only moments before going on air, panicked and got completely muddled up.

It was confusion that I could have done without, particularly as I had never been in front of a microphone before. The tent was open to the general public and, with all the noise and commotion going on behind me, I found it incredibly difficult to think, let alone talk. To make matters worse, there were also sudden and frequent outbursts of laughter that seemed to accompany my every word, which were extremely off-putting, to say the least. Only after the interview did I find out that a stray sheep had entered the tent and, much to everyone's amusement, had insisted on causing as much mayhem as possible.

Duntisbourne Leer, Gloucestershire

Reviewers, on the whole, were extremely complimentary about *The Cotswolds*. But even more pleasing was the favourable reaction from readers who took the trouble to write to us in person.

Some went to inordinate lengths, like the man from Warwickshire, who began by praising the book as 'certainly the best photographic portrayal of the Cotswold Hills that has yet appeared', then went on to give a detailed, page-by-page, analysis of the 'perfection which *might* have been achieved', commenting on such things as photographic reproduction, filters, film stocks, converging verticals, camera positions ('a better view is obtainable from further to the right'), and so on.

As Rob did not have a perspective control lens in the early days, he was only too aware of the problems of converging verticals when it came to photographing buildings. The Birthplace at Stratford-upon-Avon caused him enormous headaches. Unable to get back far enough to stop the sides of the building from leaning inwards, he had to resort to perching on top of a very tall step-ladder in order to get rid of the distortion. Furthermore, to avoid shadows falling on the frontage of the house, the photograph had to be taken during high summer, when the tourist season was at its peak.

Snapping the actual photograph may have only required a fraction of a second, but to find that perfect moment when the sun was out and the scene was devoid of milling tourists took hours. The world and his wife seemed to be visiting the property that day: posing in front of it; queuing up to get inside it; wandering round the garden; and peering through the windows.

Eventually, the moment came and Rob took the shot. Then, looking down from his elevated perch, he found that he had become a tourist attraction himself. Chattering and pointing excitedly up into the air, a coach-load of visitors were frantically taking photographs of him!

Vicars Close, Wells, Somerset

In January 1988 we started to put out feelers for a book on *Shakespeare's Avon*, the world-famous river that rises in the village of Naseby, Northamptonshire, and passes through the historic towns of Warwick, Stratford, Evesham and Pershore before merging with the Severn at Tewkesbury, Gloucestershire.

A publisher was found and contracts signed almost immediately. The hitch was that we had to deliver material for both the 'Avon' and the 'Lakes' books by the end of August 1988, for publication in Spring the following year. Working on two projects at the same time, one close to home and the other a long distance away, meant that Rob could maximize his chances of getting the best out of the capricious English weather.

How often had he set out for the Lake District in brilliant sunshine, only to find the mountains ringed by a hat of cloud? Now at least, when there was sun at home, he could take full advantage of it, being able to reach some pre-planned location anywhere on the length of the Avon within an hour at the most. The combined ploy of sticking his head out the bedroom window and/or ringing the Lakeland weather service seemed to confuse Rob's weather-Jonah completely and, for once, he was able to make good progress on both books.

Rob and I celebrated the final day of photography for *The English Lakes* by climbing Scafell Pike, which at 3,210 feet above sea-level is the highest mountain in England. We made 'the dash' from the Midlands and found ourselves in the car park at Wasdale Head at seven-thirty on a dull, but promising morning.

There are a number of routes to the summit of the mountain. Rob, true to form, chose the shortest. Anticipating a long and arduous climb, I tried to conserve my energy, stopping frequently to catch my breath while pretending to admire the view. Rob was only too happy to humour me.

When we finally reached the top, it was like a holiday camp, with almost as many people strewn over the surface as there were boulders. The massive circular stone cairn, marking the peak – which Rob wanted to photograph *without* people – proved to be the main attraction. Everyone wanted to stand on the top and pose as if they had just climbed Everest.

While waiting my turn, I took full advantage of the long and welcome rest.

The photography and research for *Shakespeare's Avon* was unusual in that it involved travelling every which way up and down the river apart from under it. Ironically, the least productive method was by boat; the banks were so high that, invariably, only the tops of church steeples could be seen.

Holy Trinity Church and River Avon, Stratford-upon-Avon, Warwickshire

The most unusual view was from above. So Rob found himself in a Jet Ranger helicopter, strapped in and sitting where the door used to be, with nothing between him and the ground but the rushing air and his trusty motor-driven Nikon camera. The noise was so loud that he had to wear a headset to communicate. Unable to use a tripod, he found that his years as a sports photographer proved invaluable. Although the camera was moving and not the subject, by using shutter speeds of a 500th of a second plus, together with anticipation, timing and rapid changes of film, he was able to rattle through shot after shot almost faster than the helicopter could roar through the sky. Flying above almost all of the Avon's 100-mile length in a helicopter was an experience that Rob, in particular, will never forget.

Features that seemed clear in the air, however, proved infuriatingly difficult to locate on the ground. A day or so after the flight, I set out to locate the source of the Avon at Naseby. But found it impossible because of the countless number of springs in the area. What I did discover, however, sent a shiver down my spine.

Having just finished writing about the ghostly re-enactment of the battle of Edge Hill, in which the phantom armies of Charles I and Parliament appeared to terrified countrymen on Christmas Eve 1642, I was well aware that, at Naseby, three years later, another Civil War battle had taken place; one in which the Royalists were decisively defeated.

Although the weather had started fine, by the time I reached Naseby, black clouds had rolled in across the sky, reducing visibility alarmingly. The atmosphere was thick and heavy, almost electric, and torrential rain seemed imminent.

Pulling up at the side of the road, I saw a sign pointing to the Cromwell Monument, one of two memorials in the area that commemorate the battle. Realising that further research would have to be abandoned once it began to rain, I decided to get out of the car and make a dash for the monument which stood at the edge of a field, two or three hundred yards away, almost on the spot where the fiercest fighting had taken place.

Halfway across the field a flash of lightning illuminated the ink-black sky, followed by a distant rumble of thunder. Trying to push the idea of ghosts and phantom armies to the back of my mind, I started to run, spurred on by the thought that if caught in the storm I'd end up drenched to the skin, or worse struck by lightning.

The shiver came, not from seeing a ghost, but from discovering a newly-laid wreath beside the monument, reading the inscription, and realising that the battle had taken place on the 14 June, the same day *exactly* as the one on which I had, unknowingly, decided to visit the site!

Source of the River Avon, Naseby, Northamptonshire

Our fifth book proved to be very different to those that had gone before. Although featuring the landscape of Shropshire and the Welsh Marches, *Cadfael Country* was based on Ellis Peters' chronicles of Brother Cadfael, the fictional twelfth-century monk and herbalist of Shrewsbury Abbey, who, more often than not, found himself solving murder mysteries.

For both of us, *Cadfael Country* turned out to be something in the nature of a pilgrimage. By following in Cadfael's fictitious footsteps we found ourselves exploring a landscape that was not only accurately described in the chronicles (allowing for the changes that had taken place since the twelfth-century), but one that was particularly rich in legend and history.

Churches, abbeys, castles, ancient towns and villages, although substantially altered, or even ruined or deserted, still managed to retain something of the essence of Cadfael's medieval world. Characters, real and imagined, seemed to come alive in our minds: Cadfael riding a mule through the remnants of the Long Forest; Prior Robert Pennant striding arrogantly down the nave of Shrewsbury Abbey with his aspirations set on becoming abbot; and Roger de Montgomery, the great and powerful Marcher lord, standing on the ramparts of one of his border castles surveying a fraction of his vast domain.

As *The Cadfael Companion*, the follow-up to *Cadfael Country*, did not require photographs, Rob was able to concentrate exclusively on our third book in the 'Country Series', *The Yorkshire Moors & Dales*.

Towards the end of 1989, however, his weather-Jonah decided to obscure the sun behind a seemingly permanent blanket of cloud, thus ensuring that for almost three long and frustrating months Rob was unable to use his cameras.

It was during this time that Rob decided to do something he had been toying with

George, near Semer Water, North Yorkshire

for a good few years. Although his knowledge of dogs was nil, he went out and unintentionally bought a particularly wilful border collie, called George, who had been abandoned in the streets of a nearby town and ended up in a dog-rescue home, run by the Canine Defence League. What Rob was hoping for was a companion, a faithful friend that would share in his photographic adventures and offer a little welcome company on lonely expeditions. If the truth were known, being somewhat of a loner by nature, he had this romantic vision of roaming the Yorkshire hills with his camera gear on his back and a loving and obedient sheepdog by his side. What he had not reckoned on was that George – wily, intelligent and street-wise – had other ideas.

Right from the outset, their relationship developed into a battle of wills. It was a struggle that went on for many months, with Rob thinking that he had won, only to find that George had simply been humouring him.

Before commencing photography on the Yorkshire book, Rob exchanged his medium-format Pentax camera for a Fuji GX680. The advantage was that the lens could be moved vertically to get rid of converging verticals, or tilted in its mount to shift the plane of focus and thereby increase the depth of field. Its only real disadvantage was its weight. But for the superhuman Rob that, surely, was not going to be a problem!

Tolhurst Farm, near Smarden, Kent

By the time the sun had decided to emerge from its enforced winter hibernation, Rob was feeling fairly confident about taking George away with him on location for the first time. George, however, being a townie, proved to be entirely ignorant of the ways of the Yorkshire countryside. Rob, prudently, kept him on a lead where sheep and cattle were concerned. But when it came to simple things, like getting over a dry-stone wall, George was hopeless. He got wedged in a stile, and was so frightened about walking over the cracks in the limestone pavement at Malham Cove that he was reduced to crawling along on his belly. He also developed the disgusting habit of not only rolling in sheep dung, but consuming it in quantity.

Even worse, while walking the hills near Keld, George discovered the rotting carcass of a sheep and, before Rob could react, had dived headfirst into it, getting lengths of putrefying intestine tangled in his fur in the process. Rob's attempts at trying to call him away fell on seemingly deaf ears, or ears filled with something indescribably disgusting. When George eventually did decide to respond, Rob found himself regretting that he had ever opened his mouth. To his horror, the creature running towards him was no longer George, but some Gorgon-like monster, with lengths of sheep's intestine writhing about on its head like living snakes. Beloved sheepdog or not, Rob was left with little choice, but to turn and flee!

Guy's Cliffe, near Leamington Spa, Warwickshire

By the time we began work on *The Heart of England* (covering Warwickshire, Hereford and Worcester, Staffordshire, Shropshire and part of Gloucestershire) our working relationship had settled down into a pattern that would last for future projects. Rob, accompanied by George, would go off to explore the landscape, town and country alike, with a view to taking scenes that would make good photographs. I, quite independently, would research, visit, check and re-check locations in order to make sure that the text was accurate. Back at home, we would regularly meet up to log photographs, compare notes and discuss current projects.

At one logging session, Rob could not contain his excitement. A shot, taken on his usual colour stock, of a ruined mansion at Guy's Cliffe, near Warwick, had turned out strangely unreal. It was almost as though it had been shot on infra-red film. The building, in silhouette, was almost black-and-white, while the foreground consisted of eerie pale grasses.

Rob had to confess that, while taking the photograph, he had felt curiously ill at ease. Despite the proximity of a busy road, there was not a sound to be heard. The river was still, the trees were motionless, and a mist covered the dark, mysterious shell of the building like a shroud.

Wheal Betsy, Mary Tavy, Dartmoor, Devon

He set up his camera and was just about to press the button, when – as if triggered by some supernatural force – a powerful shaft of sunlight burst through the mist to pierce the glassless windows of the ruins and illuminate the scene.

Despite my scepticism, Rob maintained (and still does to this very day) that, at that precise moment, lurking somewhere in the shadows of the ruins, he saw a ghostly figure. One that he was convinced had been captured in the photograph!

While Rob was chasing shadows at Guy's Cliffe, I was chasing an elusive whipping post at Eardisland, near Leominster. Having very quickly learnt that not everything that appeared in print was necessarily accurate (that wrong information very often regurgitated itself as one writer drew on the research of another), I found it imperative to verify facts for myself. In one extreme case, near Grosmont in the North York Moors, I had resorted in desperation to measuring the height of Falling Foss by means of a weighted line dropped from the top of the waterfall.

Likewise, the whereabouts of the whipping post at Eardisland had to be determined. One authority claimed that it stood on the south bank of the River Arrow, another, on the north. The more I read, the more the post kept whipping about. Only by visiting the village in person did I confirm that the post was on the south side of the river, attached to a cottage, and had, in ignorance of its historic function, been painted the same colour as the beams and timbers.

For George each trip away from home was an adventure. While Rob was busily engrossed in taking photographs for *The West Country*, George always managed to find something to keep himself amused: on Dartmoor he obligingly herded a group of curious ponies out of shot; at Clovelly he insisted on chasing the milkman's sled all the way down to the bottom of the hill; and he also made the problems of finding accommodation almost impossible.

George – being George – simply could not be relied on to behave. At Tintagel he declared war on the landlady's cat and created so much noise and chaos that Rob was forced to beat a hasty retreat. While at Newquay he accumulated so much water and sand in his coat that their bedroom at the Bed and Breakfast was very nearly transformed into Fistral Beach.

The ideal solution seemed to be a camper van. Not only would it would serve as a mobile home-from-home, but it would also offer Rob the added bonus of being able to park and sleep close to the following morning's location.

Unfortunately, Rob's first foray away in his new 'second-hand' vehicle turned out to be ill-fated. The granite rock, near where he parked on Dartmoor, must have contained a fragment of kryptonite; for, while carrying his gear across fairly easy terrain, his superhuman strength suddenly deserted him (alas, never to return), and he ended up undergoing prolonged treatment for a painful and badly strained back. The injury also meant that his medium-format Fuji GX680 had to be exchanged for a much lighter, less bulky alternative, a Mamiya 6.

Pier and Seafront, Eastbourne, East Sussex

Our sixth book in the 'Country Series' was *Wessex*, covering Wiltshire, Hampshire, Dorset, Somerset and Avon. For each of the books in the series we tried to develop a theme. With *The Cotswolds* it was the harmony and beauty of the oolitic limestone, ranging in colour from honey-gold to silver-grey. For *The English Lakes* it was the Romantic Lake Poets and the spectacular mountain scenery. *The Yorkshire Moors and Dales* celebrated the contrast and variety in the landscape; from open, heather-clad moorland and flower-rich hay meadows to high, coastal cliffs and flat, emerald plains. *The Heart of England* concentrated on the region's rich architectural heritage, together with its wealth of literary and historic associations. *The West Country* focused on the granite rock, as well as the two National Parks of Exmoor and Dartmoor. And, for *Wessex*, it was the exceptional proliferation of mysterious and mystical sites. While Rob was exploring the photographic potential of ancient – and not so ancient – chalk hill figures, carved out of the turf (notably the Cerne Abbas Giant and the white horse of Westbury), I embarked on a symbolic quest for the Holy Grail, reputed to be somewhere at Glastonbury, 'the holiest ground in England', where geomancers maintain that 'heavenly and earthly currents meet in terrestrial harmony'.

In addition to being plagued by his weather-Jonah, Rob found his battery-operated medium-format camera very unreliable. Unlike his ever-enduring Nikon, the plastic case was unable to withstand the knocks and bumps that came about through constant use; and the lenses, although extremely sharp, were very prone to flare. Reluctantly, therefore, before starting *The Garden of England,* our seventh book in the 'Country Series', he exchanged it for a mechanical Hasselblad 503CX with Hasselblad lenses.

It may be appropriate to celebrate the tenth anniversary of our partnership with a prestigious book on England, but there are still large areas that we have yet to cover, notably East Anglia and the Fens, the Peak District and Northumbria.

Covering an area of just over 50,000 square miles, England is the largest of the three territories that together constitute the island of Great Britain. Yet in comparison to other countries around the world it is tiny; its size is a mere fraction of Australia and almost a quarter of France. In fact, square mile for square mile, it would fit into the American state of Texas over five times.

Barber Stone, Avebury, Wiltshire

The ever-changing coastline, deeply indented with jutting headlands, small coves, broad bays and sweeping estuaries, is some 2,000 miles long, with the highest cliffs being in the south-west (Exmoor, in fact, where they reach nearly 1,000 feet). At its closest point, near Dover in the south-east, England is just over twenty miles from the European mainland, to which it was once joined. The highest mountains and the largest lakes occur in the north-west, while the lowest land, some of it below sea-level, is found in the east and the south-east. Dividing northern England into north-east and north-west are the Pennines, a chain of limestone hills that stretch northward for some 250 miles from Derbyshire to Northumberland. London, England's largest city, is not only the nation's capital, it is also the capital of the United Kingdom.

Despite the fact that England is densely populated and heavily industrialized, it is renowned for the rich diversity of its landscape, especially in relation to its small size. Less than eight percent of the total land surface, however, has been designated a National Park; the largest, the Lake District, covers an area of 885 square miles, while the smallest, Exmoor, is a mere 265 square miles.

Sadly, despite the protection offered by such powerful conservation bodies as the National Trust, English Heritage and the National Park authorities, many of the nation's finest landscapes are being destroyed by the effects of pollution, popularity, litter and vandalism. Right from the outset, Rob's photographs have been unashamedly promotional, aiming to represent each location at its very best. But it is proving difficult to maintain the celebratory nature of his work. Unsightly foam gathers at the foot of waterfalls and along the banks of fast-flowing rivers, all manner of objects – not necessarily of marine origin – wash up on beaches, discarded bottles, cans and plastic bags intrude almost everywhere, and even the air is often contaminated by a thick and lingering haze.

Bluebell Wood, Stoneleigh, Warwickshire

In these times of expanding ugliness, when all that we cherish is being threatened by desecration, it is our sincerest hope that, in some small measure, the books we produce may inspire respect for the vanishing beauty of the landscape and nurture an awareness of the preciousness of the environment.

For, to paraphrase the statesman and historian, Winston Churchill, a nation which destroys its heritage, deserves to have no future.

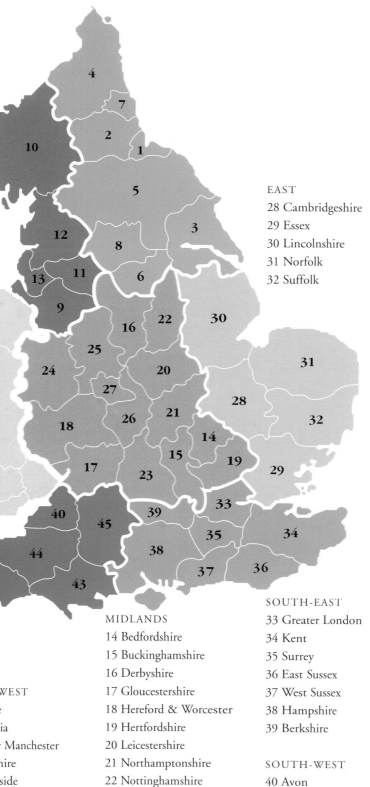

EAST
28 Cambridgeshire
29 Essex
30 Lincolnshire
31 Norfolk
32 Suffolk

NORTH-EAST
1 Cleveland
2 Durham
3 Humberside
4 Northumberland
5 North Yorkshire
6 South Yorkshire
7 Tyne and Wear
8 West Yorkshire

NORTH-WEST
9 Cheshire
10 Cumbria
11 Greater Manchester
12 Lancashire
13 Merseyside

MIDLANDS
14 Bedfordshire
15 Buckinghamshire
16 Derbyshire
17 Gloucestershire
18 Hereford & Worcester
19 Hertfordshire
20 Leicestershire
21 Northamptonshire
22 Nottinghamshire
23 Oxfordshire
24 Shropshire
25 Staffordshire
26 Warwickshire
27 West Midlands

SOUTH-EAST
33 Greater London
34 Kent
35 Surrey
36 East Sussex
37 West Sussex
38 Hampshire
39 Berkshire

SOUTH-WEST
40 Avon
41 Cornwall
42 Devon
43 Dorset
44 Somerset
45 Wiltshire

▶ Rudland Rigg, North Yorkshire

The belief that fairies and goblins inhabited the remoter parts of the North York Moors – especially prehistoric monuments like those found on Rudland Rigg, above Farndale – were prevalent in the countryside until well into the nineteenth century. One such hobgoblin, for example, called Obtrusch, who lived in a tumulus (or round barrow) on Rudland Rigg, made life so unbearable for one Farndale farmer that he determined to leave. 'Ah see thoo's flittin!', said a neighbour, meeting him on the road, but it was a cheeky goblin's voice that responded: 'Aye, we's flittin!' The farmer returned home; there was no point in going if the hobgoblin was to follow him.

Of all England's traditional landscapes the north-east offers some of the finest examples of both natural and man-made scenery, boasting as it does three contrasting National Parks: the North York Moors, the Yorkshire Dales, and Northumberland, designated in 1952, 1954 and 1956, respectively.

Covering an area of 553 square miles, the North York Moors embraces a thirty-five-mile-wide upland swathe of wild heather moorland, cut by rich, green valleys and deep, dramatic ravines, bounded to the east by the high cliffs of the North Sea coast and to the west by the steep escarpments of the Cleveland and Hambleton Hills.

Stretching for some 30 miles between the Pennines and the Vale of York, the Yorkshire Dales National Park encompasses an area of 680 square miles, most of which lies in North Yorkshire. Traditionally, however, the Dales embrace a much larger area than that defined by the Park boundaries. In broad terms, they stretch north to the Tees, south to the Wharfe, west to the Lune and east to the Vale of York. Limestone is the predominant feature of the central and south-western Dales. The scenery in the northern Dales is characterized by a combination of lush green pastures, dry-stone walls and isolated field-barns.

The Northumberland National Park, covering 398 square miles, has a long and irregular boundary that stretches north for some 45 miles from Hadrian's Wall towards the Scottish Border. Situated in one of the most remote and least populated areas of England, the landscape is dominated by hills that rise gradually in height through farming dales and heather moors to the Cheviots. Running along the southern edge of the Park (and, beyond, to the Farne Islands) is the Great Whin Sill. Formed of a hard molten basalt or dolerite, it provides the natural foundations for Hadrian's Wall and the coastal fortresses of Dunstanburgh and Bamburgh.

Much as there is to celebrate about the English countryside, very few areas are entirely 'natural'. The north-east, because of its long and troubled history of border conflict, is littered with military relics, the greatest being Hadrian's Wall. Built by the Romans almost 2,000 years ago, it has now become such an integral part of the natural and man-made scenery of northern England that it would be hard to imagine the countryside without it.

◄ Lindisfarne Castle, Northumberland

Linked to the mainland by a mile-long causeway, passable only at low tide, the Holy Island of Lindisfarne was one of the most important centres of Celtic Christianity in England. The first monastery on the island was founded by St Aidan, an Irish monk of Iona, who was invited to preach in Northumbria shortly after the convert Oswald became king in 635. The most famous of the Lindisfarne bishops, of which Aidan was the first, is St Cuthbert, who died in 687 and was buried on the island. In 875 hostile incursions by the Vikings forced the monks to abandon the island, taking with them the relics of Cuthbert (now in Durham) and the Lindisfarne Gospels (now in the British Library). The priory, founded by Benedictine monks from Durham in the late eleventh century, was dissolved in 1537. The castle, built in the sixteenth century as a Border fortress, was converted in 1903 by Sir Edwin Lutyens into a country residence for Edward Hudson, founder of the magazine *Country Life*.

▲ Bamburgh Castle, Northumberland

In 547 Ida, King of Bernicia (the northern half of the Anglo-Saxon kingdom of Northumbria), built a fortress on the craggy outcrop at Bamburgh. Ida's grandson, Ethelfrith, King of Northumbria from 593 to 616, gave the fortress to his wife Bebba. Thereafter, the settlement was known as Bebba's Burgh or Bebban-burgh, from which the name Bamburgh is derived. After the Norman Conquest the castle was rebuilt in stone as a Border fortress – against incursions by the Scots. During the Wars of the Roses it was captured by Edward IV. and became the first castle in England to fall to artillery fire. In 1610 the property was given by James I of England (James VI of Scotland) to Claudius Forster, whose descendants allowed the castle to fall into decay. It was purchased in 1704 by Nathaniel Crewe, Bishop of Durham, and was subsequently restored. Further restoration and rebuilding were carried out towards the end of the nineteenth century by the Victorian inventor and industrialist William, the 1st Lord Armstrong, whose family still own the property.

▶ Durham Cathedral and River Wear, Durham

Dominating the ancient city of Durham, the cathedral and castle stand side by side on a steep, rocky peninsular almost islanded by the River Wear. The city's ecclesiastical history begins in 995 with the arrival of a community of monks, originally from Lindisfarne, bearing the body of St Cuthbert and the head of St Oswald. Today the remains of both saints lie under a plain marble slab behind the High Altar of the Norman cathedral. The building also contains the bones of the Venerable Bede (d. 735), which were smuggled out of the monastery at Jarrow and taken to Durham in about 1022. Founded shortly after the Norman Conquest, the castle was eventually transformed from a fortress into the main residence of the Prince Bishops of Durham. In 1837 it became the home of University College, part of the University of Durham. The Old Fulling Mill, below the cathedral's two 144-feet west towers, now houses a museum run by the University Department of Archaeology.

▲ Dunstanburgh Castle, Northumberland

In 1312 Piers Gaveston, the homosexual lover of Edward II, was executed by order of Thomas, 2nd Earl of Lancaster, the leader of baronial opposition to the king. The following year, faced with the threat of royal reprisal as well as Scottish invasion, Lancaster started to build a powerful fortress on an eminently defensible site at Dunstanburgh, enclosing some eleven acres. Although the earl received a royal pardon for his part in Gaveston's death some eight months after work on Dunstanburgh had begun, his relationship with the king, his cousin, was always strained. In 1315, the year following Edward's disastrous defeat by Robert the Bruce, King of Scotland, at Bannockburn, Lancaster became virtual ruler of England. In 1322 Lancaster was captured by Edward at the Battle of Boroughbridge, and, after a summary trial, he was executed as a traitor. John of Gaunt (1340–99) carried out various alterations and additions at Dunstanburgh in the 1380s, including the construction of a second gatehouse east of that built earlier by Lancaster.

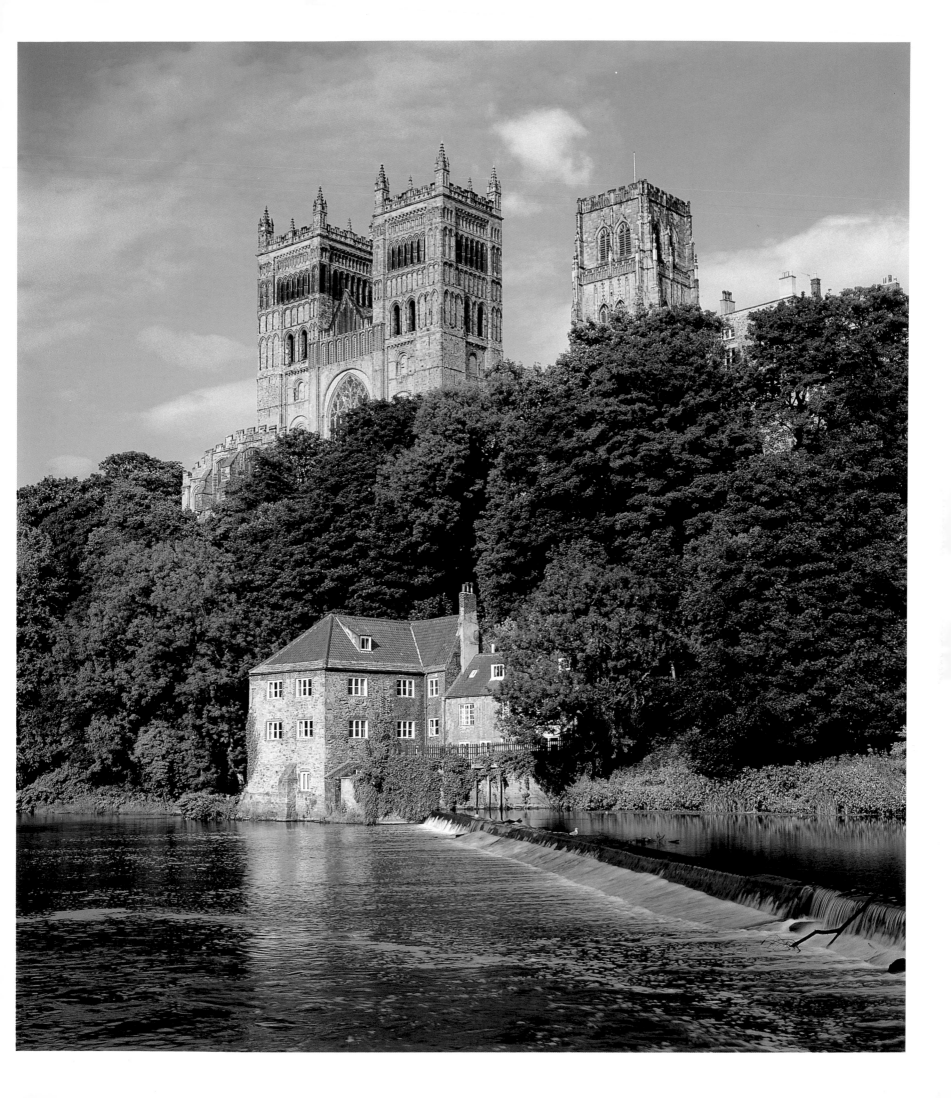

◄ Barnard Castle, Durham

Perched high on a cliff overlooking the fast-flowing River Tees, the ruins of Barnard Castle stand on the site of a small earth-and-timber fortification built by Guy de Baliol in 1095. Guy's nephew, Bernard de Baliol I, succeeded to the estate in about 1125 and began work on transforming the small fortress into one of the largest stone castles in the north of England. Outside the walls, he laid out a town which, like the castle, came to be named after him. Apart from a few short interruptions, the Baliol family held the castle until 1296, when John de Baliol, crowned King of Scotland in 1292, was captured by Edward I and his English estates were confiscated. In 1307 ownership of the castle was granted to Guy de Beauchamp, Earl of Warwick. A Crown possession from 1481 until 1603, the castle gradually fell into decline, and in 1630 it was partly demolished by Sir Henry Vane to provide materials for the rebuilding of Raby Castle. The remains, including the Round Tower of c. 1200, which still stands some forty feet high, are now in the care of English Heritage.

► High Frith, West Stones Dale, North Yorkshire

Parts of the wild, rolling moorland beyond upper Swaledale, notably along the valley of the Stonedale Beck (or West Stones Dale), have been enclosed by dry-stone walls. Characteristically, many of the enclosures contain large stone field barns, strategically placed to allow the hay crop to be swept directly into them. Today, however, many of the barns have fallen into disrepair or been made redundant, because of modern changes in farming practices. In this remote wilderness farming remains entirely pastoral, with sheep predominating over cattle. Despite the coming of the railway and the establishment of mining communities, brought about by the Industrial Revolution in the nineteenth century, sheep remain a vital part of the economy and evolution of the landscape. It is not surprising, therefore, that the head of a Swaledale ram should have been chosen as the emblem of the Yorkshire Dales National Park.

▲ River Swale, near Keld,
Upper Swaledale, North Yorkshire

Although the headwaters of the Swale rise on the peaty, moorland heights of the hills which divide North Yorkshire from Cumbria, the river actually begins at the point where the Birkdale Beck meets the Great Sleddale Beck, some two miles upstream of Keld. Set amidst wild crags and bleak mountain scenery, the former lead-mining village – with its sandstone houses, post office, chapel and youth hostel (formerly a shooting lodge) – occupies a remote headland above the swift-flowing river. The name 'Keld' is, in fact, an old Norse word meaning 'a place by a river'. The Pennine Way passes within a few hundred yards of the village, and many walkers make the detour for rest and refreshment. In the vicinity of Keld, the Swale has cut through the layers of limestone to produce an impressive collection of waterfalls: Kisdon Force is considered the most dramatic; while East Gill Force, on a small tributary of the Swale, is one of the most attractive, with water cascading over a series of stepped ledges.

▲ Kisdon Hill, near Muker,
North Yorkshire

The Corpse Way – an ancient green track once used mainly for carrying the bodies of the dead down Swaledale – climbs steeply from Keld up the western side of Kisdon before crossing the hill and descending to Muker. Before 1580, when a new chapel and burial ground were consecrated at Muker, all the corpses in upper Swaledale were buried in the parish churchyard at Grinton, nine miles further down the valley. According to T.D. Whitaker, a nineteenth-century historian, the bodies were carried upon the shoulders of men, 'not in coffins but in rude wicker baskets'. Since 1832, when the commons of Kisdon were enclosed, drystone walls and field barns have been a feature of the 'island' hill.

▶ River Swale, Upper Swaledale,
North Yorkshire

From its endless trickling origins, high up on the Pennine moorland of Birkdale Common, Angram Common and Stonesdale Moor, the River Swale plunges eastward to Keld, tumbling over a series of dramatic falls and through a wooded limestone gorge, before sweeping south in a long, sinuous 'S' bend to Muker. On its twenty-mile journey eastward from Muker to Richmond – the 'Gateway to Swaledale' – the river passes through scenery characteristic of much of the Dales: lush green water meadows, flower-rich hay pastures, traditional field barns and dry-stone walls, all surrounded by steep, grassy hillsides, scarred in places by the abandoned debris of lead mining. Beyond Richmond, the Swale meanders south-eastward through the Vale of York to join the Ure, two miles east of Boroughbridge. The photograph was taken from near the ruins of Crackpot Hall, looking south to Muker Common.

◄ Field Barns, near Gunnerside, Swaledale, North Yorkshire

Most of the stone-walled fields in upper Swaledale contain a large, two-storeyed stone barn in which to store hay and house cattle over the winter months. Depending on the area, the names for the barns vary: in Swaledale they are called 'field barns' or 'cow houses'; while in Wharfedale and Craven they are called 'laithes'. In the two-mile stretch between Gunnerside and Muker there are literally hundreds of barns, most of which were built when the land was enclosed in the late eighteenth and early nineteenth centuries. The combination of dry-stone walls and field barns is a distinctive feature of the Dales landscape and it is found nowhere else in Britain. Until 1580 (when burial ground became available at Muker), the graveyard at Grinton was the only consecrated ground in upper Swaledale. Consequently, corpses were carried for burial along the Old Corpse Way – a twelve-mile track from Keld to Grinton by way of Muker, Gunnerside, Feetham, Healaugh and Reeth.

◄ Lower Aysgarth Falls, Wensleydale, North Yorkshire

From its source on the Pennine heights of Abbotside Common, the River Ure flows south-eastward down Wensleydale to the Vale of York, where – like the Aire, Wharfe, Nidd and Swale – it joins the Ouse eventually to debouch into the North Sea by way of the Humber estuary. Wensleydale, however, unlike all the other major Dales, is not named after the river that runs through it. Instead, it takes its name from the ancient village of Wensley ('Waendel's forest clearing'), situated just outside the eastern boundary of the National Park. Near Aysgarth, in upper Wensleydale, the Ure cascades over a series of broad limestone steps, or terraces, to create one of the most famous waterfalls in the country. In fact, within one half-mile stretch of the river at Aysgarth there are three sets of falls: the Upper (immediately above the narrow, single-arched stone bridge); and the Middle and Lower (below the bridge), both of which are reached by a woodland footpath running alongside the north bank of the river.

▲ Askrigg and Addlebrough, Wensleydale, North Yorkshire

Situated on the north bank of the River Ure, midway between Aysgarth and Hawes, the grey, stone village of Askrigg – for centuries an unofficial trading centre – had its market status confirmed by charter in 1587. Thus Wensley's position as the commercial hub of Wensleydale was usurped, but Askrigg, in turn, lost its importance to Hawes, higher up the Dale, when the latter was granted its first market charter in 1700. Askrigg's decline was further exasperated when the turnpike road from Richmond to Lancaster – authorized in 1751 – was re-routed through Hawes in 1795. Most of the buildings in Askrigg date from the eighteenth and nineteenth centuries, when the village flourished on industries such as textiles, clock-making and hand-knitting. For the BBC television series *All Creatures Great and Small*, Askrigg became 'Darrowby'; and Skeldale House (formerly Cringley House), near the old market cross and parish church, became the surgery-home of the country vet James Herriot.

◄ **Deepdale, North Yorkshire**

Deepdale, a tributary valley of Dentdale, is dominated by the soaring heights of Whernside (2,419 feet) and Great Coum (2,250 feet). The Deepdale Beck, which flows north through the valley, rises on the western slopes of Yorkshire's highest mountain to join the River Dee less than a mile above the small township of Dent. Near Sedburgh, the waters of both rivers merge with the Lune, eventually entering the Irish Sea near Lancaster. Many of the fields and pastures in Deepdale and Dentdale are separated by hedgerows rather than the traditional dry-stone walls of the more easterly Dales. Dent, with its stone houses and cobbled streets, is a popular centre for walkers. Although knitting as a cottage industry was popular in many of the Dales until the end of the nineteenth century, the output of the inhabitants of Dentdale was so fast and so furious that they came to be known as the 'Terrible Knitters of Dent'.

◄ **Whernside, from White Scars on the western slopes of Ingleborough, North Yorkshire**

The Yorkshire Dales has more 'limestone pavement' than any other part of Britain. This distinctive rock formation was created after Ice Age glaciers had scoured parts of the landscape down to bare limestone, exposing a network of thin surface cracks, or joints, which were widened and deepened by rainwater over time to form fissures, or 'grykes', that vary in width from a few inches to several feet. The limestone blocks, forming the pavement top, are known as 'clints'. And the erosive action of running water is responsible too for a vast unseen network of potholes, passages and caverns beneath this strange landscape. The distant peak in the photograph is Whernside (2,419 feet), the highest mountain in Yorkshire.

▲ Watlowes Dry Valley, near Malham, North Yorkshire

Millions of years ago a massive upheaval in the earth's crust caused a major east-west fracture, known as the Mid-Craven Fault, in which rocks to the south slipped, dropping away vertically to reveal the cliff-face of Malham Cove – some 300 feet high. At one time Ice Age meltwater flowed down the deep, steep-sided Watlowes Dry Valley (above the cove) to cascade over the cliff in a spectacular fall, higher than Niagara. The beck, which now emerges from the crack at the base of the cliff, comes from a stream that sinks underground near Smelt Mill Chimney, one-and-a-half miles north-west. Watlowes, although cut by glacial meltwater, has no stream running through it. Above Malham Cove (to include Watlowes) is an extensive area of limestone pavement. Gordale Scar, just over a mile to the east, is a deep, narrowing gorge of towering, limestone cliffs. And at the head of the gorge, which terminates in a dark and eerie amphitheatre, a beck pours through a natural hole in the rock wall to create a series of small waterfalls.

◀ Danby High Moor, North Yorkshire

The main watershed, running from east to west across the North York Moors, is centred on the expansive block of heather- and bilberry-covered moorland around Danby High Moor, some 1,400 feet above sea level. The streams draining north descend through a series of deep valleys – Westerdale, Danby Dale, Great Fryup Dale and Glaisdale – to join the River Esk. Those heading south flow through several larger and longer valleys – Bransdale, Farndale and Rosedale – eventually to enter the River Derwent, a tributary of the Ouse, near Selby. Separating the valleys, and radiating out like the spokes of a giant wheel, are a succession of descending ridges, or riggs: Castleton Rigg, Danby Rigg, Glaisdale Rigg, Northdale Rigg,

Blakey Ridge and Rudland Rigg. Over three thousand years ago many of these ridges were occupied by prehistoric people, and even today there is still abundant evidence of their barrows, burial mounds and rectangular enclosures.

▲ Fat Betty, Danby High Moor, North Yorkshire

Of all the hundreds of marker stones and crosses found scattered throughout the North York Moors, by far the most famous are the group on Danby High Moor, near Rosedale Head, known as Fat Betty, the Margery Stone, Old Ralph and Young Ralph. There is a legend which seeks to account for the stones' presence in the landscape, as generally there tends to

be with stones or objects whose origins lie shrouded in mystery. Ralph, an aged lay servant at the small Cistercian nunnery in Rosedale (founded some time before 1158) escorted Sister Elizabeth high up onto the moors to meet Sister Margery of Baysdale. Unfortunately, a thick fog descended without warning and the parties became lost. While Elizabeth waited beside a large rock, where she knelt and prayed for many hours, Ralph set off to find Margery. When the fog eventually cleared, Elizabeth climbed on top of the rock and was able to see both Ralph and Margery, a short distance away, and not far from each other. Their positions are now marked by the stones. Young Ralph is a more recent arrival, probably dating from the eighteenth century.

▲ Sandsend Beach, near Whitby, North Yorkshire

Sandsend, a small seaside resort of inns, cottages and hotels, lies at the foot of Lythe Bank, and at the north-western end of the long, sandy beach which stretches some three miles to Whitby. The village itself is divided by two parallel streams that rise deep in the heart of Mulgrave Woods. East Row, at the Whitby end of the village, overlooks the East Row Beck; while Sandsend itself, with its small Victorian church, stretches up both sides of Sandsend Beck. In September 1994 the sinking of the yacht Akiba hit the national newspaper headlines and created a frenzy of activity along the coast around Whitby. People who seldom visited beaches like Sandsend suddenly found an excuse to be down by the sea. In the circumstances they should not have been surprised to find themselves under constant surveillance by HM Customs officers, for the yacht, lost whilst being towed into port, was carrying a valuable and illegal cargo – two tons of Moroccan black cannabis resin, broken down and sealed in manageable watertight packages, and rumoured to be worth five million pounds.

▶ Whitby Harbour, North Yorkshire

The ancient fishing town of Whitby, at the mouth of the River Esk, grew and prospered in the seventeenth and eighteenth centuries when alum – mined inland and along the coast – was shipped out of the port. From 1753, for some eighty years, it was an important whaling base, sending in one season as many as twenty ships to the icy waters of the Arctic. Boat-building in the town dates back at least to medieval times, probably earlier, and Captain James Cook, who moved to the port from Staithes in 1746, used Whitby-built ships for his epic voyages of discovery. Although as a major port Whitby has declined, a small fishing fleet is still maintained, and in 1979 a 200-berth yachting marina was also opened. Esk, the dredger in the photograph, was designed to carry 150 tons

of mud and silt from the harbour out to sea. High on the are the sandstone ruins of Whitby Abbey, founded in AD 657 by St Hilda. Meanwhile, the parish church of St Mary, close by, dates from the twelfth century.

▲ Wrecked boat, Saltwick Bay, near Whitby, North Yorkshire

The east coast of England holds the record for the greatest number of shipwrecks in Britain. Literally thousands of ships have been lost on the rocks on the Yorkshire coast alone, rent asunder by the treacherous ferocity of the

North Sea storms. At Saltwick Bay, east of Whitby, the wrecks include the Rohilla, a Red Cross hospital ship of 7,409 tons, bound for Dunkirk to take on wounded soldiers during World War I. Tragically, on the night of 29 October 1914, a violent storm smashed the ship onto a reef. Out of a total of 229 on board, 149 were rescued by the heroic courage of lifeboat crews. Bram Stoker, author of Dracula (1897), chose this part of the coast as the setting for his fictional Count's arrival in England. It is possible that Stoker may have been inspired to make Dracula take the form of a black dog by the Whitby legend of the Barguest, a monstrous hound with glowing red eyes. The terrifying creature, reputed to stalk the narrow streets and alleys of the port at night, was feared by the inhabitants as a harbinger of death.

▶ Falling Foss, Little Beck Valley, North Yorkshire

From its source amidst the forest plantation which now covers Sneaton High Moor, the May Beck flows south to plummet over the fifty-foot precipice of Falling Foss and into the wooded ravine of the Little Beck. The way-marked walk which begins near the waterfall follows the Little Beck downstream to the Hermitage, before returning up the opposite side of the valley to Falling Foss and Midge Hall, from whence there is the option to take a longer, circular walk up the May Beck Valley. The Hermitage, a shelter hollowed out of solid sandstone, is said to have been carved by a man called Jeffrey, who also carved two small seats on the top. The inscription 'G.C. 1790' above the door refers to George Chubb, a schoolmaster from the near-by village of Little Beck. The derelict Midge Hall, just above the waterfall, was originally a gamekeeper's cottage, and later a museum. Traces can still be found of the outdoor toilet which not only emptied into the fall, but was strategically positioned almost directly over it!

▲ Egton High Moor, from Murk Mire Moor, North Yorkshire

One of the most gruelling walks across the North York Moors is the forty-mile Lyke Wake Walk, established by Bill Cowley in 1955. Starting from near Osmotherley, and finishing at Ravenscar, walkers face the challenge of completing the high moorland crossing in under twenty-four hours. Those who accomplish this feat are entitled to join the Lyke Wake Club. The name of the walk was taken from the ancient Cleveland Lyke Wake Dirge, a dialect verse which suggested that after some-one died, their soul would make its final journey across the moors. 'Lyke' means corpse, while 'wake' means the watching over of a corpse. There are a number of accepted alternative routes across the Moors, one of which avoids the Early Warning Station of Fyling-dales Moor by heading north from Hamer across Egton High Moor. Apparently, membership to the club is open not only to deserving walkers, but also to those who manage to accomplish 'a ski crossing in twenty-four hours' daylight'.

▼ Robin Hood's Bay, North Yorkshire

The Yorkshire fishing village of Robin Hood's Bay – with its tightly packed, red-pantiled houses and network of narrow alleyways descending steeply from the cliff top to the very edge of the North Sea – was once a notorious haven for smugglers. Despite various legends about Robin Hood in the locality, there is no proof that the village (often called Bay Town, or simply Bay) had any connection with the medieval outlaw. In 1780 many of the cottages along King Street, the original main street, slid into the sea. After a further landslip in 1791, it was decided that 'New Road' be built, the present, steep main street, at the foot of which are the oldest buildings. Further development took place higher up the slopes in the nineteenth century, due to a growth in population, increased wealth from the fishing industry and the arrival of the railway in 1885. Without a harbour, however, the size of boat was extremely limited and, as a port, Bay inevitably declined. To protect the village from the erosive action of the sea, a sea-wall forty feet high was constructed in 1975.

▲ Horn Ridge and Blakey Ridge, from Rudland Rigg, North Yorkshire

Belonging entirely to the Jurassic period, the rocks of the North York Moors were formed by horizontal layers of sediment settling on the bed of a tropical sea more than 140 million years ago. This sea bed – composed of layers of shale, sandstone and limestone – was then forced upwards and tilted towards the south by cataclysmic movements in the earth's crust. Later, the erosive effect of wind and rain, together with numerous and sometimes dramatic changes in the climate, shaped and moulded the hills and valleys. Glacial action during the Ice Ages smoothed the surface of the hills, deepened the valleys, and deposited clay, boulders and stones. Natural forces, however, were not entirely responsible for the present landscape. Much of the transformation of what was once a forest into open heath, grassland, cultivated fields and conifer plantations is due to man's presence.

▶ Saltergate Moor, North Yorkshire

Almost half of the North York Moors National Park is covered by wide expanses of heather, and as such it is the largest area of open heather-covered upland in England. Blossoming in August and September and grazed by sheep throughout the year, the growth of the heather is managed by controlled burning, or 'swiddening', which takes place between November and March when the peat is damp, thereby preventing the roots of the plant from being destroyed. The young green shoots, produced after the old woody heather has been burnt, provide essential nourishment for both sheep and grouse – both an important part of the moorland scene. The heather also provides a source of nectar for the bees of local bee-keepers, who put hives out on the moors.

◀ Farndale, North Yorkshire

Each spring in Farndale the banks of the River Dove are festooned with wild daffodils, known also as 'Lenten Lilies'. Once in danger of being wiped out by irresponsible visitors, the flowers are now protected by law; indeed, 2,000 acres of the 'Daffodil Dale' has been designated as a nature reserve since 1953. Although there are three small but distinct hamlets in the Dale – Church Houses, Low Mill and Lowna – much of the long, steep-sided valley is occupied by scattered farmsteads. It was once a busy mining centre. Jet, coal, ironstone and gravel all used to be worked in the Dale, or on the high moors above it. During the 1930s – and again in the 1960s – it was feared that a proposed reservoir would flood the upper valley, but after vehement protests the plan was dropped. High up at the southern end of Farndale stands the upland village of Gillamoor, with a 'surprise view' over-looking the valley. The parish church there was built by one man, James Smith, in 1802, and restored in 1880.

◄ Hutton-le-Hole, North Yorkshire

Lying in a green hollow on the southern edge of the North York Moors, the ancient village of Hutton-le-Hole was owned by the Benedictine monks of St Mary's Abbey at York until the Dissolution. Recorded in the Domesday Book simply as 'Hotun', meaning 'the place near burial mounds', the present name dates from the 1800s and was originally 'Hutton Underheg', or 'Hutton under the Park Boundary'. The Hutton Beck, rushing through the middle of the long, undulating village green, rises on the heather-clad wilderness of Spaunton Moor eventually to join the Derwent and Ouse. The oldest buildings in the village date from the seventeenth century, when many of the Quaker families wove woollen cloth in their own homes. Many re-erected traditional buildings have been preserved at the Ryedale Folk Museum in Hutton-le-Hole. Some of the hearth beams are held up by 'witch posts', carved with a cross and blessed by the priest, to protect the occupants from the evil powers of witches.

► Handstone, Spaunton Moor, North Yorkshire

The oldest routes across the Moors were those that avoided the soft valley bottoms and kept instead to the high, firm ridges. These ancient ridgeways were often marked with stones, variously known as waymarkers, guide stones or, if carved with a hand, handstones. The handstone in the photograph is situated some two miles north of Hutton-le-Hole, on the east side of the Blakey Ridge road, and was probably erected in the early eighteenth century. Running along the ridge beside the stone is a narrow, deeply worn track, known as a 'hollow way', many of which date back to prehistoric times. The stone-flagged causeways, or 'trods', laid across boggy moorland to provide dry passage for heavily laden packhorses, date from medieval times. Some were established as monastic routes, linking abbeys to outlying granges, but others – if one believes their names – were attributed to smugglers, Quakers and panniermen. Many lead to medieval bridges, such as Beggar's Bridge at Glaisdale and Duck Bridge at Danby.

▶ Village and Church of All Saints, Helmsley, North Yorkshire

Straddling the southern border of the North York Moors National Park, and at the convergence of major roads from York, Pickering, Stokesley and Thirsk, the ancient town of Helmsley is centred round a spacious market square, in the middle of which is a canopied monument to William, 2nd Lord Feversham (d. 1867). The market cross, close by, originally stood in the graveyard of All Saints' parish church, tucked away behind the houses, shops and hotels of the square. Although the Domesday Book of 1086 records a church at 'Elmeslac', or Helmsley, only fragments of the Norman church remain, incorporated into the present edifice, which was built between 1866 and 1869, in the style of the thirteenth century. The ruins of the castle, standing on the site of an earlier stronghold, date from the end of the twelfth century. Strategically situated on an outcrop of rock on the north bank of the River Rye, immediately west of the town, the castle was besieged by the Parliamentarians in 1644 and, after its capture, was partly demolished.

▶ Hambleton Hills Escarpment, from Whitestone Cliff, North Yorkshire

The Hambleton Hills – overlooking the Vale of York at the western edge of the North York Moors – stretch roughly from Sutton Bank in the south to Hambleton End, above Thimbleby Moor, in the north. The ridgeway (known as the Hambleton Road) running along the crest of the hills is part of an ancient highway linking Scotland with the south of England. During the eighteenth and nineteenth centuries the road was used by Scottish drovers bringing cattle to market at York and Malton. But moving cattle long distances on foot declined with the arrival of the railways, and indeed ceased completely at the beginning of the twentieth century. Lake Gormire, at the foot of the steep escarpment of Sutton Bank, was formed in the Ice Age when a glacial meltwater channel was partly blocked by a landslide. One legend claims that the lake is bottomless; another that it is haunted by a white horse and its rider who fell to their death from the top of Whitestone Cliff (or White Mare Crag) above.

▶ **Loughrigg Tarn,
near Skelwith Bridge, Cumbria**

Situated at the foot of Loughrigg Fell's south-western side, Loughrigg Tarn is privately owned, with no public access. In 1811 it was part of the estate of Sir George Howland Beaumont, Bart., friend and patron of William Wordsworth. In 1811 the poet called it Diana's Looking Glass in a poem; thirty years later he explained why: 'Loughrigg Tarn ... resembles ... the Lake Nemi, or Speculum Dianae as it is often called, not only in its clear waters and circular form, and the beauty immediately surrounding it, but also as being overlooked by the eminence of Langdale Pikes as Lake Nemi is by that of Monte Calvo.'

In his guide to the Lakes, written in the early nineteenth century, William Wordsworth summed up much that is still true of the region:

I do not indeed know any tract of country in which, within so narrow a compass, may be found an equal variety in the influences of light and shadow upon the sublime or beautiful features of landscape.

His vision became a reality in 1951 when the Lake District was designated a National Park. Covering an area of 885 square miles in the centre of Cumbria, it is the largest National Park in Britain. It also contains England's highest mountain, Scafell Pike at 3,210 feet, and sixteen lakes including Windermere, as well as countless tarns.

The Lake District is rich in history and tradition, and out of the working life of the dalesman has grown a number of distinctly Cumbrian sports, all of which require great strength and stamina: fell running, wrestling, hound trailing and fox-hunting (not on horseback but on foot). In 1975 Jos Naylor, a sheep farmer from Wasdale, set an awesome record by climbing seventy-two Lakeland peaks in less than twenty-four hours. Incredibly, in June 1988 the record was broken by a Cheshire computer programmer, Mark McDermott, who added a further four summits to Naylor's total: achieving an astounding seventy-six summits within the time limit – a total of almost 40,000 feet of ascent and descent and a distance equivalent to the combined heights of Scafell Pike, Ben Nevis, Snowdon and Everest!

The Lakeland landscape is particularly celebrated for its inspiring influence on such literary figures as Wordsworth, Coleridge and Southey, known as the Lake Poets. Among the many other writers and poets associated with the region is Beatrix Potter – Mrs Heelis, as she preferred to be called – whose tales of Peter Rabbit, Mrs Tiggy-Winkle and Jemima Puddleduck have delighted generations of young children since her first illustrated book was published in 1901.

Despite its comparatively small area and the fears by many that industry and tourism would destroy the unique character and exceptional beauty of the scenery, the Lake District has not been ruined. Certainly, the landscape and our perceptions of it have changed over the centuries. But its uplifting effect on the hearts and minds of millions, makes the region one of the most precious of all the jewels in England's resplendent crown.

▼ Over Water, near Uldale, Cumbria

The countryside around the small farming village of Uldale, on the remote northern fringe of the Lake District National Park, comprises open moorland, gentle, rolling hills, lush pastures and unfenced roads, across which wild fell ponies can wander freely. The distinctive peak in the middle of the photograph is Skiddaw, the fourth highest mountain in Lakeland at 3,053 feet above sea level. Although there are no lakes at the 'back o' Skidda', a small beck runs down from the moorland fells to flow through Little Tarn and Over Water before feeding into the Chapelhouse Reservoir, where it emerges as the River Ellen. Over Water (just visible in the middle distance of the photograph) is less than a quarter of a mile long. In the cemetery of St Kentigern's church at Caldbeck, north-east of Uldale, are the graves of Mary Harrison, née Robinson – 'The Maid of Buttermere' – who died in 1837, and John Peel, the legendary huntsman, who spent a lifetime sounding his horn and wakening the dead.

▶ Loweswater, Cumbria

Lying in a secluded valley north-west of Crummock Water, Loweswater – just over a mile long, half a mile broad and sixty feet deep at its maximum – is unique, for it is the only one of the sixteen lakes whose waters flow inward towards the centre of Lakeland. Its outlet, the Park Beck, heads in a south-easterly direction to Crummock Water, whence it emerges as the River Cocker to flow north through the Vale of Lorton to Cockermouth and the Derwent. The parish church of St Bartholomew at Loweswater – situated between the two lakes in the middle of a flat, fertile alluvial plain – dates from 1827, but was almost entirely rebuilt in 1884. The work is thought to have been undertaken in a spirit of optimistic anticipation inspired by the opening of a lead mine at nearby Godferhead. In the event, the mine failed and the population (which was expected to increase significantly) remained static. Hidden among the trees of Holme Wood (on the right of the photograph) is a small waterfall: Holme Force.

◄ Buttermere and Crummock Water, from Fleetwith Pike, Cumbria

With its rich meadows and wooded shores, Buttermere (the nearest lake in the photograph) is enclosed by a magnificent amphitheatre of steeply sloping rock: from the north-eastern shore the fellside soars to the summit of Robinson; while on the opposite side a rugged mountain wall rises to the triple peaks of the High Stile range; and Fleetwith Pike and Haystacks stand at the head of the valley. Rising from the deep hollow of Warnscale Bottom, Haystacks was regarded by Alfred Wainwright (1907–91) with special affection. In *A Pictorial Guide to the Lakeland Fells: Book Seven*, he wrote: 'For a man trying to get a persistent worry out of his mind, the top of Haystacks is a wonderful cure.' Spilling down the fellsides, numerous streams wash soil and rock down into the valley – especially after storms – and the resulting silt is deposited in the gradually widening plain that separates Buttermere from Crummock Water (at one time one large lake). Crummock Water (the distant lake) is almost double the size of Buttermere.

▲ Derwentwater and Jaws of Borrowdale, Cumbria

The 'Queen of the Lakes', Derwentwater is four miles long, one and a quarter miles wide and seventy-two feet deep at its deepest. In addition to its four main islands – Derwent Island, Lord's Island, St Herbert's Island and Rampsholme Island – there is a floating 'island', which appears every three years or so; it is really a mass of weeds and rotting vegetation brought to the surface by marsh gases. The River Derwent, from which the lake takes its name, rises on the soaring heights above the lush Borrowdale valley. Flowing north, it is suddenly constricted by the narrow, steep-walled, thickly wooded gorge known as the Jaws of Borrowdale, beyond which it becomes wide and shallow before entering Derwentwater. Passing through Bassenthwaite Lake and Cockermouth, where Wordsworth was born, the river eventually reaches the Irish Sea at Workington. Behind the Lodore Hotel at the southern end of the lake one of Lakeland's most popular waterfalls – the Lodore Falls – is to be found.

◄ **Hindscarth and Robinson,
Newlands Valley, Cumbria**

Separating the lush and fertile pastures of Newlands Valley from the western shore of Derwentwater is a range of fells, which rise from Cat Bells (1,481 feet) to High Spy (2,143 feet). The upper valley has three branches, each with its own stream: Newlands Beck, the main river, rises on the heights of Dale Head, Hindscarth and High Spy, to flow north into Bassenthwaite Lake; Scope Beck originates on the slopes of Little Dale, the high valley lying between the summits of Hindscarth and Robinson; while the source of the Keskadale Beck lies between Robinson and Knott Rigg, on Buttermere Moss. Little Town, with its small white-washed church of Newlands, lies near the confluence of the three becks. It was hereabouts, at 'the back of the hill called Cat Bells', that Beatrix Potter set *The Tale of Mrs Tiggy-Winkle* (1905).

► **Whelpside Gill, Thirlmere, Cumbria**

The massive Helvellyn range towers above Thirlmere, its western slopes dropping steeply into the dense conifer plantations that fringe the lake's artificial shores. Numerous streams tumble from the mountain slopes, helping to feed the reservoir with pure, clean water, which is then piped almost a hundred miles to industrial Lancashire at the rate of millions of gallons each day. The long, low chapel of Wythburn stands, hidden by trees, near the foot of Whelpside Gill; it is the starting point for the popular 'Wythburn' route up Helvellyn – at 3,118 feet, the third highest mountain in Lakeland. About a mile north of the chapel, just beyond 'Straining Well' pumping station, is the original site of the famous 'Rock of Names' (now at the Wordsworth Museum), where Dorothy and John Wordsworth, Mary and Sara Hutchinson and Coleridge carved their initials.

▲ Honister Quarry,
Honister Crag, Cumbria

From Seatoller (reputedly the wettest inhabited place in England), the Borrowdale road from Keswick climbs steeply to Honister Pass, before descending into the Buttermere valley. Honister Crag, a towering cliff overlooking the boulder-strewn pass, has been industrially quarried for its attractive green volcanic slate since at least the mid-seventeenth century. The crag is honeycombed by a vast labyrinth of tunnels that penetrate into the very heart of the rock at different levels. Conditions for the quarrymen were both primitive and dangerous. Right up until the twentieth century they were expected to work by candlelight. Accidents were frequent, hours were long and wages were low. The finest quality slate was located near the top of the crag and, before the introduction of gravitational railways in the late nineteenth century, the stone was brought down by sled, with a quarryman running in front. The photograph was taken at the Road End entrance of the abandoned workings. The rails (two feet wide) once carried trucks into and out of the underground tunnels, while the cabins were used for rest and shelter.

◄ Ullswater, from Glencoyne Wood, Cumbria

Seven and a half miles long, about three quarters of a mile wide and over 200 feet deep, Ullswater is the second largest of the sixteen lakes. Serpentine in shape, its three distinct reaches mark the gradual transitions from wild mountain scenery to gentler, less spectacular countryside: the head of the lake lies in the rugged rocks of the Borrowdale volcanic group, its middle in the low-lying slate of the Skiddaw group; and its foot in the rounded hills of the Mell Fell conglomerate. Beyond, in the flat plain of the River Eamont, which flows out of the northern end of the lake, a belt of carboniferous limestone stretches north-eastward towards Penrith. In the late eighteenth century the lake's peace was often broken by the sound of cannons, deliberately discharged – in the words of William Gilpin – 'for the purpose of exciting echoes'. He also suggested, as an alternative, that a few French horns and clarinets be introduced to 'form a thousand symphonies, playing together from every part'.

▲ High Street, from Racecourse Hill, Cumbria

The highest Roman road in Britain – linking the legionary forts of Galava (Ambleside) with Brocavum (Brougham, near Penrith) – climbs high up onto the far eastern fells and runs along the long whale-backed crest of High Street (approximately 2,700 feet above sea level). Probably in use long before the arrival of the Romans, the ancient route was known as Brettestrete or 'the Britons' road' in the thirteenth century. Until the early nineteenth century the smooth, verdant slope of High Street was used by the farmers of Mardale (the valley to the east) as the venue for their annual meet. The original purpose of the autumn gathering was to allow the shepherds to retrieve or identify any stray sheep, though later it became a great festive occasion with horseracing, wrestling, fell running and other sports among the attractions. Barrels of beer and large quantities of food were carried up from the valley to the lofty arena. Eventually the meet was transferred to the Dun Bull Inn at Mardale, but its life there was short; the annual fairs finally ceased in 1935, the same year that the last service was held in Mardale church.

▶ Grasmere Island, Grasmere, Cumbria

The little lake of Grasmere has a single island, where Dorothy and William Wordsworth used to picnic. Often, when he wanted solitude, the poet would row out to the island, sometimes sharing the stone barn with the sheep and cattle for which it provided shelter. The following was 'written with a pencil upon a stone in the wall of the house (an outhouse) on the island at Grasmere in 1800':

'Thou see'st a homely Pile, yet to these
        walls
The heifer comes in the snow-storm,
        and here
The new-dropped lamb finds shelter
        from the wind.
And hither does one Poet sometimes
        row and beneath this roof
He makes his summer couch, and here
        at noon
Spreads out his limbs, while, yet
        unshorn, the Sheep
Panting beneath the burthen of their
        wool
Lie round him, even as if they were a
        part
Of his own household.'

▲ Grasmere, from Red Bank Woods, Cumbria

One summer holiday, when he was still a schoolboy, Wordsworth was mysteriously drawn to the little vale of Grasmere. Later he wrote of the experience in his unfinished poem 'The Recluse', vowing that '... here Must be his Home, this Valley be his world.' On 20 December 1799, at the age of twenty-nine, his childhood dream was fulfilled when he and his sister Dorothy moved into Dove Cottage: 'And now 'tis mine, perchance for life, dear Vale, Beloved Grasmere (let the Wandering Streams Take up, the cloud-capt hills repeat, the Name), One of thy lowly dwellings is my Home.' He was to live at Grasmere for the next thirteen years: first at Dove Cottage, and then at Allan Bank and, finally, at the Old Rectory. As he was an energetic walker, often covering up to thirty miles in a day, the entire vale and surrounding fells were familiar to the poet. The white building in the photograph is the Prince of Wales Hotel, where Wordsworth launched and landed his boat when he lived at Dove Cottage.

◀ Dove Cottage, Town End, Grasmere, Cumbria

William Wordsworth's first home at Grasmere was the small, dark and low-ceilinged cottage at Town End; he moved there with his sister Dorothy in 1799. During the Wordsworth's residency, the 'lowly dwelling' did not have a name. Only later did it become known as 'Dove Cottage', and that was because is was originally an inn called the Dove and Olive Branch. Thomas de Quincey, who had set out to see Wordsworth on two occasions, but turned back because his courage failed him, finally met the poet at Dove Cottage on 4 November 1807; the event is described in his Recollections of the Lakes and the Lake Poets. Despite Wordsworth's great happiness with the place, the cottage eventually became too cramped for the family (which had grown, to include not only Dorothy and William, but his wife Mary and their three children, plus Sara Hutchinson [Mary's sister] and a host of visitors and friends). In 1808 they moved across the vale to Allan Bank. De Quincey took over the tenancy of Dove Cottage and remained there with his family for almost twenty years. The property is now owned by the Wordsworth Trust and is open to the public.

▶ Rydal Water, Cumbria

Lying in the deep, steep-sided valley of the River Rothay between Ambleside and Grasmere, Rydal Water is just three-quarters of a mile long, a quarter of a mile wide and only fifty-six feet at its deepest. The lake was originally named Routhermere or Rothaymere after the river, but got its present name from the village situated at its eastern end. Rydal Mount, a large house on the wooded hillside above the chapel (now church) of St Mary, was Wordsworth's home from 1813 until his death on 23 April 1850, at the age of eighty. It takes its name from the ancient mound or mount – once a beacon site – located beyond the gravel forecourt of the house. From the summit there is a distant view across Windermere to Belle Isle and Bowness beyond. In 1825 the poet purchased a plot of land next to the newly erected chapel with the intention of building his home there should he be evicted from Rydal Mount. He eventually gave the land, which he had planted with daffodils, to his daughter Dora. Now known as Dora's Field, it is owned by the National Trust.

▲ Rydal Water, from White Moss Common, Cumbria

Dorothy Wordsworth often wrote in her journal of the frequent journeys on foot that she and William made, from Town End, Grasmere, to Rydal to collect their mail. The route took them up the hill from Dove Cottage to White Moss Common from where there is a splendid view over Rydal Water:

'This is White Moss, a place made for all kinds of beautiful works of art, nature, woods and valleys, fairy valleys and fairy tarns, miniature mountains, alps above alps.'

White Moss, lying between the two lakes of Grasmere and Rydal Water, rises from the flat, wooded alluvial plain of the River Rothay. The elevation takes its name from the cotton-grass which thrives in the wet, swampy ground found thereabouts. When in flower the plant seems to be covered with balls of pure white cotton wool. Rydal Water, smaller than some of the tarns, is also the second smallest of the sixteen lakes.

◄ Castlerigg Stone Circle, Keswick, Cumbria

Dramatically situated on a high plateau (700 feet high), and surrounded by a ring of high fells, including Blencathra, Skiddaw and Helvellyn, Castlerigg Stone Circle is thought to be over 3,500 years old, dating from the late Neolithic or early Bronze Age. At the turn of this century it was popularly – and incorrectly – believed to have been built by the Druids as a temple in about the first century BC. When Wordsworth and Coleridge added their names to the long and eminent list of visitors to the 'Druids Circle' during their walking tour in 1799, they found that the stones had been painted white. The circle was purchased in 1913, by Canon Rawnsley and others on behalf of the National Trust. The circle is oval in shape, about 100 feet in diameter, and comprises thirty-eight roughly hewn stones with, unusually, a further ten forming a rectangle on the east side. The largest stone is over seven feet tall and weighs several tons. Like the stone circles of Swinside, near Broughton-in-Furness, and Long Meg and her Daughters, near Salkeld, the purpose of Castlerigg remains a mystery.

**▲ River Brathay in flood,
near Skelwith Bridge, Cumbria**

Rising on Pike o' Blisco, the River Brathay flows eastward through Little Langdale Tarn and Elterwater to the Roman fort of Galava near Waterhead, where, after merging with the Rothay, it enters the northern end of Windermere. At Skelwith Force, near Skelwith Bridge, the Brathay is squeezed through a narrow cleft of rock. After heavy rain – despite a drop of only fifteen to twenty feet – the waterfall carries what is possibly the greatest volume of water in the Lake District. At such times the two-mile stretch of the Brathay below Skelwith often floods, turning the valley into one vast lake. Tradition holds that at the approach of the spawning season, the char and trout of Windermere swim upstream together to the confluence of the Brathay and the Rothay. There the fish separate, the char going west up the Brathay to Elterwater, and the trout going north up the Rothay to Rydal Water. Scientific investigation, however, has found that there are trout – but not char – in both the Brathay and the Rothay, and that there are two distinct populations of char in Windermere, both spawning in the lake at different depths and at different times.

▲ **Elterwater,**
from the north-east shore, Cumbria

Situated at the junction of the Great and Little Langdale valleys, the shallow, irregular-shaped lake of Elterwater is fed by the waters of the River Brathay and the Great Langdale Beck. Only half a mile long and a quarter of a mile wide, it is the smallest of the sixteen lakes and, like many of the others, it is gradually getting smaller because of the accumulation of silt and other river-borne materials. The infilling process has been steady and continuous since the last glaciation, and has already been responsible for removing at least one lake further up the valley in Great Langdale. Green slate has been quarried in the area for centuries and in 1824, north of Elterwater village, gunpowder mills were established, powered by water from Stickle Tarn (which was dammed especially for the purpose) and the Great Langdale Beck. Charcoal came from the surrounding woodlands, while saltpetre and sulphur were brought by boat – either up Coniston Water or up the River Brathay from Windermere – and was then transported overland. The mills closed in 1928–9.

◄ **Little Langdale,
from Wrynose, Cumbria**

As Little Langdale is shrouded in mist rising from the valley bottom, so the history of the area is riddled with tales of mystery: tales of smugglers and the exploits of the notorious Lanty Slee who, during the mid-nineteenth century, operated several illicit distilleries in hideouts high up in the fells around Wrynose. One such hideout was in a cave in the long-abandoned quarry of Betsy Crag, below Low Fell on Wetherlam. In *Inside the Real Lakeland*, A.H. Griffin described the cave where he discovered the remains of Lanty's apparatus, including the 'spring where he obtained his water', 'pieces of the pipe which carried the exhaust steam back into the water', the 'ashes of his last fire' and 'cunningly concealed beneath the floor at the back of the cave … his store place – probably his whisky store'. Although some of Lanty's whisky was sold locally, most of it went over the old smugglers' road to the port of Ravenglass. Lanty died in 1878 at Greenbank Farm, Little Langdale, aged seventy-six.

▲ **Bleatarn House and Lingmoor Fell,
from Pike O'Blisco, Cumbria**

Lingmoor Fell, a crescent-shaped ridge of high ground reaching 1,530 feet above sea level, separates Great Langdale from Little Langdale. Linking both valleys is a narrow, winding road that climbs the side of the bracken- and heather-covered fell to pass Bleatarn House, the home of Wordsworth's 'Solitary' ('The Excursion: Book II'). In the poem the stone farmhouse is described as 'one bare dwelling; one abode, no more!', and the nearby tarn as 'a liquid pool that glittered in the sun'. Like Bleatarn House, many of the farmsteads, barns and dwellings in the Lake District are built of stone and slate, quarried locally on a small scale. North-west of the farmhouse the road zigzags steeply down into Great Langdale, where the 'two huge peaks' of the Langdale Pikes – the 'prized companions' of the 'Solitary' – rise abruptly from the Mickleden Valley. Pike o' Blisco (the fell from which the photograph was taken) rises to 2,304 feet above sea level, and can be easily climbed from Wrynose Pass.

▲ Eskdale, from Hardknott, Cumbria

In the valley below the remains of Hardknott Roman Fort, the River Esk rises to its source near Esk Hause, which, at 2,490 feet, is the highest foot pass in the Lake District. From the pass, which descends into Borrowdale, a track climbs steeply, westward, past Calf Cove, Ill Crag and Broad Crag, to the rubble-strewn summit of Scafell Pike. Strictly speaking, Scafell Pike should be called Scafell Pikes, as it comprises three 'principal' summits, each more than 3,000 feet: Ill Crag (3,040 feet); Broad crag (3,054 feet); and Scafell Pike itself (3,210 feet). The Scafell range, which includes Scafell Pike, is part of a huge amphitheatre of towering fells that dominate the head of Eskdale. Not surprisingly, the valley, which has no lake, is noted for its diversity of landscape: from the rocky grandeur of England's highest mountains to the green meadows and woodlands of the plain, and the sandy mud flats of the estuary. It is also noted for its miniature steam railway, officially called the Ravenglass & Eskdale Railway, but affectionately known as 'La'al Ratty'.

◄ Hardknott Roman Fort, Hardknott, Cumbria

Almost 2,000 years ago the Romans built a military road from the port of Glannoventa (Ravenglass) to the fort of Galava (Ambleside). Passing through some of the highest and wildest country in England, the route from the coast (at Ravenglass) followed the valley of the River Esk eastwards, corkscrewing upwards through the passes of Hardknott and Wrynose, before dropping down into Little Langdale, the Brathay valley and Ambleside. Near the summit of Hardknott – some 1,291 feet up – at the head of Eskdale and below the high rocky crags of Border End, the Romans established one of the loneliest outposts in their entire empire; it was called Mediobogdum, which meant 'the fort in the middle of the bend'. Designed to hold a cohort of 500 men, it was built during the reign of the Emperor Hadrian (AD 117–138) and was garrisoned by soldiers from Dalmatia in eastern Europe.

► Sunset over Irish Sea with tidal marker, near Ravenglass, Cumbria

Situated near the confluence of the rivers Irt, Mite and Esk, Ravenglass was once a busy Roman supply base, a medieval market town, a ship-building settlement and an infamous haunt of smugglers. Today, however, Ravenglass is no longer the important port it once was, and its natural harbour has almost silted up. Less than half a mile south of the settlement, the Romans built a stone fortress on a cliff overlooking the Irish Sea. Although little survives of this fort, the remains of a Roman bath house, known locally as Walls Castle can be found a little way to the east. Approximately forty feet wide and ninety feet long, it used to have everything from hot saunas to cold baths. With walls some twelve feet high in parts, the bath house is the tallest surviving Roman building in the whole of northern England, and one of the best preserved in the country. The long duneland peninsula to the north-west of Ravenglass is a nature reserve with a variety of habitats, including freshwater pools, sandy shores, tidal flats and salt marshland.

◄ Coppermines Valley, Coniston, Cumbria

In the Coppermines Valley, approximately two miles north-west of the village of Coniston in the valley of the Red Dell Beck, the scattered remains of old mine workings scar the open fellside. Evidence shows that the Company of Mines Royal mined here towards the end of the sixteenth century, employing German and Austrian labour. Most of the crumbling ruins date from the nineteenth century, however, when hundreds of men were engaged to tunnel into the rock – back-breaking work. The dark, often waterlogged entrances to the deep underground shafts – which descend to many different levels – are in an extremely dangerous and dilapidated condition and should not be entered. Traces can be found on the surface of almost every stage in the processing of copper ore, from the distinctive waste heaps to the ruins of sheds, shafts and engine houses.

► Yew Tree Farm, Coniston, Cumbria

Considered by Beatrix Potter to be 'a typical north-country farmhouse, very well worth preserving', Yew Tree Farm is just one of over eighty working Lakeland farms now in the care of the National Trust. Dating from the seventeenth century or earlier, its most celebrated feature is the open 'spinning gallery' attached to the barn, which was used not only for spinning, but for storage, for drying wool, and as a means of access to the upper storey of the building. The farmhouse has been whitewashed, a fashion that Wordsworth hated. He recommended instead that if a house must be painted then it should be painted to blend in with the landscape, and not 'materially impair the majesty of a mountain.' The most famous and most visited farmhouse in Cumbria is undoubtedly Hill Top at Near Sawrey, where Beatrix Potter wrote and illustrated many of her books. When she died in 1943 she owned fourteen farms, numerous cottages and 4,000 acres of land. She left it all to the National Trust.

◄ Levens Hall, Kendal, Cumbria

One of the largest Elizabethan houses in Cumbria, Levens Hall dates from the latter half of the thirteenth century, when it was owned by the de Redman family. The original house, with its medieval pele tower and hall, was completely remodelled by the Bellinghams from about 1570 to 1590, while the South Wing and the Brewhouse were added by Colonel James Grahme in the late seventeenth century. It was Grahme who commissioned Monsieur Guillaume Beau-

mont, gardener to King James II, to design and lay out the grounds. Beaumont's crowning achievement was the topiary with its staggering variety of geometrical Alice-in-Wonderland shapes, all clipped from yew and beech, with box forming the borders of the flower beds. Planted in 1692 and beautifully maintained in its original plan, the topiary is reputed to be the oldest in England. Now owned by the Bagot family, the house, park and gardens - five miles south of Kendal - are open to the public.

► Bowness Bay,
Bowness-on-Windermere, Cumbria

Situated in the middle reaches of the east shore of Windermere, opposite Belle Isle, Bowness-on-Windermere is Lakeland's largest holiday resort, and a popular centre for boating activities. Steamers operate from the pier in Bowness Bay throughout the season, and there is a regular ferry service across the lake. Although Bowness and Windermere are joined together, they are, in fact, two separate towns: Bowness, despite the predominance of Victorian houses and hotels, dates from at least Anglo-Saxon times; while Windermere developed out of the little village of Birthwaite after the arrival of the railway in 1847. Belle Isle is named after Isabella Curwen, who purchased the island and its unique Georgian round house in 1781. Some three miles north of Bowness, the Lake District National Park Visitor Centre at Brockhole – with grounds running down to the eastern shore of the lake – was originally the country home of a nineteenth-century Lancashire cotton magnate.

▶ **Looking south-west from the side of Pontesford Hill towards Wales, Shropshire**

Seven miles south-west of Shrewsbury, near the former mining village of Pontesbury, are the 'Pontesbury Hills': Callow Hill, Pontesbury Hill, Earl's Hill and Pontesford Hill. Legend has it that hidden on Earl's Hill is a golden arrow, and whoever finds it will come into a large fortune. On Palm Sunday young people used to race up the hill to pick a twig from the haunted yew tree at the top, before searching for the golden arrow and racing back down the hill. Those that managed to dip their fourth finger into the deep pool at the bottom were destined, for good or for ill, to marry the first person of the opposite sex they met after that.

For the stranger who wanted to know something of England, Henry James advised in *English Hours* (1877), that there could be no better way than to spend a fortnight in Warwickshire. 'It is the core and centre of the English world; midmost England, unmitigated England.'

Today, literary pilgrims from all over the world are drawn to 'leafy Warwickshire' because of its connection with William Shakespeare and with Stratford-upon-Avon, the small market town of his birth – and death. Despite his pre-eminence, however, Shakespeare is but one of many writers, artists and poets who have found reason to celebrate the countryside of Middle England, renowned as it is for its historical, industrial and romantic associations. Although essentially a pastoral land of gentle, rolling hills, watered by age-old rivers like the Severn, Trent, Thames, Avon and Wye, the heartland of England has witnessed many decisive battles in the nation's history because of its strategic position – from Caratacus's heroic last stand against the Romans in AD 51 to Charles II's humiliating defeat by Cromwell at Worcester in 1651.

In the south of the region, between the university city of Oxford and the flood-plain of the tidal River Severn, are the limestone hills of the Cotswolds – famed for the colour of its underlying rock which brings beauty and harmony to every field, town and village. Buildings made from this golden, almost luminous stone, as J. B. Priestly wrote in *English Journey* (1934): 'knew the trick of keeping the lost sunlight of centuries glimmering about them.'

The Peak District, in the north, embraces the most southerly part of the Pennines, and thereby marks the transition from lowland to highland England. It has two strongly contrasting landscapes: the Dark Peak and the White Peak. Each has its own distinct character, based on the predominant rock: the former being gritstone and the latter limestone. Covering an area of 555 square miles, the Peak District National Park, created in 1951 (almost twenty years after the historic mass trespass of Kinder Scout), was the first National Park to be designated in Britain.

To do real justice to the rich heritage of Middle England, a fortnight spent in Warwickshire can only be a beginning.

◀ Ladybower Reservoir, from Whinstone Lee Tor, Peak District, Derbyshire

Submerged beneath the still, dark waters of Ladybower Reservoir, formally opened by King George VI in 1945, are the remains of Derwent and Ashopton, two lost but not forgotten Derbyshire villages. Before World War I, when the reservoirs of Howden and Derwent were constructed to supply water to the growing industrial towns of Sheffield, Nottingham, Derby and Leicester, only a few isolated farms in the upper Derwent valley were destroyed. The villages of Derwent and Ashopton remained unaffected until the construction of a third dam across the valley at Ladybower in the 1930s. Sometimes, when the waters are abnormally low, the ruins of Derwent reappear. Ashopton, however, lies so deep under the waters that its remains are unlikely to be seen again. Howden, Derwent and Ladybower, simply known as 'the Dams', are but three of over fifty reservoirs in the National Park, and, being the largest, have been dubbed the Peak's Lake District.

▲ The Tower & Alport Castles Farm, Hope Forest, Peak District, Derbyshire

Throughout England many of the lower slopes of steep-sided hills, including the Cotswold Edge and the Lower Greensand escarpment of the Weald in Surrey, contain debris formed by ancient landslides. Two of the most impressive examples in the Derbyshire Pennines are Alport Castles, west of Derwent Reservoir, and Mam Tor, at the edge of the 'Dark Peak' near Castleton. Among the features of the former – one of the largest landslides in Britain – is the 'Tower', an isolated mass of eroded gritstone and shale that has slowly detached itself from the main cliff of Alport Castles. Although it looks like the crumbling ruins of an artificial fortress, the Tower is an entirely natural formation. Because the slopes of Mam Tor are constantly crumbling it is known as the 'Shivering Mountain'. More severe landslips, however, have led to the permanent closure of the old A625 trans-Pennine road which used to pass below the Tor.

▲ Monsal Dale Viaduct, from Little Longstone, Peak District, Derbyshire

Rising on the moorlands, west of the Georgian spa town of Buxton, the River Wye follows a south-westerly course through limestone country to Rowsley, where it joins the Derwent – a tributary of the Trent. At the hamlet of Little Longstone, some three miles north-west of Bakewell (the administrative 'capital' of the Peak National Park), the Wye flows under the stone arches of Monsal Dale Railway Viaduct, built in 1863. In 1980, twelve years after the line was closed, the track was purchased by the National Park, who converted it into the Monsal Trail footpath, eight and a half miles to link Coombs Road Viaduct (south-east of Bakewell) to Wye Dale (east of Buxton). In addition to building England's first water-powered cotton-spinning mill on the Derwent at Cromford, near Matlock, in 1771, Richard Arkwright also established two more on the Wye: Lumford Mill at Bakewell and Cressbrook Mill in Miller's Dale.

▶ Stanage Edge, near Hathersage, Peak District, Derbyshire

Stanage Edge – the long, broken wall of precipitous gritstone, which runs north for some four miles from the Cowper Stone – is one of the most popular climbing sites in England. The coarse gritstone covering the northern, western and eastern sides of the National Park was once quarried on a large scale. The stone was not only used in the construction of such famous buildings as Chatsworth and The Crescent at Buxton, but for the manufacture of grindstones and millstones too. Towards the end of the eighteenth century, however, due to the import of cheaper stone from France, the latter industry declined and eventually came to an end. Below many of the 'edges', including Stanage, Millstone and Curbar, are piles of abandoned millstones or grindstones, some roughly hewn, others almost finished. Local tradition holds that Robin Hood was born at Loxley, north-east of Stanage, and that Little John was buried in the churchyard at Hathersage.

▶ Chatsworth House, Peak District, Derbyshire

Chatsworth House, the home of the Duke and Duchess of Devonshire and the so-called 'Palace of the Peak', was begun in 1687 by William Cavendish (later 1st Duke of Devonshire) and completed in 1707. The 6th duke added the north wing in the 1820s and, between 1839 and 1841, he also built the present estate village of Edensor on the western edge of the park. Although the church of St Peter, rebuilt in the 1860s, still stands on the site of old Edensor church, the original village, which used to stretch eastward as far as the River Derwent and possibly up to the house, was depopulated when the grounds were landscaped. The Emperor Fountain, built in 1843 by the Duke's head gardener Joseph Paxton, is Britain's tallest, reaching up to over 260 feet. This bridge was designed by the architect James Paine, and built in 1762, after 'Capability' Brown had altered the river's course.

◀ Curbar Edge, near Baslow, Peak District, Derbyshire

Running for over twelve miles from Derwent Edge to Chatsworth, along the eastern rim of the Derwent valley, is a steep and almost unbroken escarpment of coarse gritstone, which includes Stanage Edge, Burbage Rocks, Froggatt Edge, Curbar Edge, Baslow Edge and Birchen Edge. On Big Moor, east of Curbar Edge, extensive Bronze Age remains survive, including stone circles, settlement earthworks, field systems and over a hundred burial cairns. To the south, separated by the Bar Brook valley and Gardom's Edge, are monuments to Nelson and Wellington, erected in 1810 (on Birchen Edge) and 1866 (on Baslow Edge) respectively. Near Nelson's Monument are three gritstone boulders, known collectively as the 'Three Ships'. The cotton mill at Calver, east of the village of Curbar, was built by Richard Arkwright in 1803–4 and became Colditz Castle in the BBC television series *Colditz*. The photograph was taken from the top of Curbar Edge looking south-eastward to Baslow Edge and Chatsworth Park.

▲ The Roaches & Hen Cloud, near Leek, Peak District, Staffordshire

North-east of the moorland textile town of Leek, the dark and dramatic buttressed ridge of the Roaches – rising to over 1,500 feet above sea level – form one of the most impressive gritstone outcrops in the whole of the Pennines. The name 'Roaches' is probably derived from the French for 'rocks'. Doxey Pool, on the broad grassy slopes beneath the ridge, is traditionally said to be the home of a mermaid. Purchased by the Peak National Park in 1979, the Roaches estate, covering almost 1,000 acres, supports a surprising variety of wildlife, including the blue or mountain hare and a small colony of red-necked wallabies, the latter being descendants of animals that escaped from a private collection at nearby Swythamley Park in the 1940s. Hen Cloud, the isolated southern extension of the Roaches, rises steeply from the moor to 1,240 feet. Lud's Church, a mile or so north-west of the Roaches, is a deep gritstone chasm created by a huge landslip. It is reputed to be the legendary Green Chapel of the medieval alliterative poem 'Sir Gawain and the Green Knight'.

▶ Severn Valley,
from Leighton, Shropshire

Rising on Plynlimon in the mountains of central Wales, the River Severn (or Afon Hafren) flows in a huge semicircular curve through Shropshire, Worcestershire and Gloucestershire to debouch into the Bristol Channel and eventually the Atlantic Ocean. Following a course of 220 miles, it is the longest river in Britain (the Thames is five miles shorter which makes it the longest river in England). The first English town on the Severn is Shrewsbury, around which the river doubles back on itself to form a tight loop. From there it winds south across the Shropshire plain to Leighton, where – before entering the narrow Ironbridge Gorge – it meanders across open, and almost treeless, water-meadows in a series of classic horseshoe bends. The village of Leighton, attractively situated on elevated ground between the wooded slopes of the volcanic hog-back of the Wrekin (1,335 feet) and the emerald fields of the Severn, is the birthplace of the Shropshire novelist Mary Webb (1881–1927).

▶ Severn Gorge,
Ironbridge, Shropshire

Heralded as the 'Birthplace of the Industrial Revolution', the four-mile stretch of the Severn between Coalbrookdale and Coalport – known as the Ironbridge Gorge – became Britain's first declared World Heritage site in 1986. It was at Coalbrookdale, in 1709, that Abraham Darby I became the first person to successfully smelt iron using coke instead of the traditional charcoal, thereby making it possible to mass produce cast-iron cheaply. His original smelting furnace still survives near the Museum of Iron, which illustrates the history of ironmaking and the achievements of the Darby ironmasters. The world's first cast-iron bridge – spanning the heavily wooded limestone cliffs of the gorge – was cast by the Coalbrookdale Comp-

any of Abraham Darby III. Designed by Thomas Farnolls Pritchard, a Shrewsbury architect, the bridge was opened on New Year's Day 1781. The town of Ironbridge, running along the northern side of the gorge, dates mainly from the eighteenth century and takes its name from the bridge.

▲ Church Stretton, from Carding Mill Valley, Shropshire

Located in the heart of Stretton Dale, between the volcanic ridge of the Stretton Hills and the wild moorland plateau of the Long Mynd, Church Stretton is celebrated more for its dramatic mountain scenery than for the town itself. After the arrival of the railway in Victorian times, it developed from a small market centre into a fashionable health resort and spa town, known as 'Little Switzerland'. The church of St Lawrence, dating from the Norman period, has an ancient fertility figure, known as a 'Sheela-na-gig', over the north doorway. One of the most popular of the deep valleys (locally called batches or hollows) which run south-east from the broad and undulating Long Mynd plateau into Stretton Dale is the Carding Mill Valley, with the Lightspout Waterfall

at its head. Although there was a mill in the valley possibly as far back as Anglo-Saxon times, the carding (wool) mill (no longer in existence) dated only from the 1820s. Its wheel, powered by water from the stream which runs down the valley, survived until about 1912.

▲ Mitchell's Fold, Stapeley Hill, Shropshire

The earliest prehistoric monuments in Shropshire date from the Bronze Age and include the numerous barrows on the Long Mynd and several stone circles, of which Mitchell's Fold, on Stapeley Hill is the best known.

Erected over 3,500 years ago, the circle is about eighty feet in diameter and elliptical in shape. Of the estimated thirty-seven stones that form the ring, only fifteen remain, the tallest of which is six feet high. According to legend, one of the stones, and almost doubtless it is the tallest, is an old witch called Mitchell, who was turned into stone by a fairy as a punishment after she had caused havoc by playing tricks on the magical cow of Stapeley Hill. The other stones in the circle were then erected to prevent her escape. The story goes that the cow had been sent to the hill daily by the fairy, in order to provide the local inhabitants with an everlasting supply of milk. By using a sieve, however, instead of a bucket, which would have filled up, the witch tricked the animal into yielding all its milk. The cow collapsed, exhausted, and vanished, never to be seen again.

▶ West Street, Pembridge, Herefordshire

Lying on the south bank of the River Arrow, the small town or large village of Pembridge is noted for its many black and white timber-framed buildings, the earliest dating from the fourteenth century. The New Inn, standing at the crossroads in the centre of the ancient market town, dates from 1311 and was originally a coaching house. In the square behind the inn is the early sixteenth-century Market Hall, its stone-tiled roof supported by eight oak pillars. Among the many other buildings of interest are: the former rectory, now a shop called 'Ye Olde Steps'; Duppa's Almshouses, founded in 1661; Trafford Almshouses, founded in 1686; and the seventeenth-century Court House Farm, which occupies the site of a moated castle or manor house. The fourteenth-century church of St Mary the Virgin has a detached, three-storeyed pagoda-like bell tower, structurally related to the Scandinavian style of timber construction adopted in Essex, but strangely out of place in the Marches.

▶ River Arrow, Eardisland, Herefordshire

Five miles west of Leominster, Eardisland on the River Arrow is said to be one of Herefordshire's prettiest villages. Although many of its houses and cottages are pleasantly spread out along the banks of the river, the early thirteenth-century church of St Mary the Virgin lies hidden, down a narrow lane to the south, near the earthwork remains of a moated castle. The old grammar school – located immediately south of the bridge, between the river and the mill stream – was built in 1652. It closed in 1825 and has now been converted into two private dwellings: Millstream and Bridge Cottages. At the end of the latter, facing the bridge, is a whipping-post to which local wrongdoers were manacled for punishment. In the grounds of the seventeenth-century manor house, near the former mill, is a tall, four-gabled brick dovecote. The superb timber-framed, sandstone-tiled Staick House, on the north bank of the river, dates in part from the fourteenth century. 'Staick' is thought to be derived from stank, meaning a river-dam.

**▲ Lower Brockhampton, near
Bromyard, Herefordshire**

Situated between the Malverns in the east and the Black Mountains of Wales in the west, Herefordshire – watered by rivers like the Wye, Lugg, Monnow, Arrow and Teme – is essentially an agricultural county. William Camden noted in his Britannia, first published in 1586, that the county was renowned for its three Ws – wheat, wool and water. A fourth could be added – wood – for Herefordshire, in Pevsner's words, 'is one of the timber-using counties *par excellence.*' Timber-framed buildings can be found in abundance and one of the most attractive is the manor house at Lower Brockhampton. It dates from the end of the fourteenth century and has the added bonus of a rare fifteenth-century, detached gatehouse straddling the moat. Built by John Domulton, a descendant of the Brockhampton family who lived here from at least the twelfth century, the house was partially rebuilt in the 1870s. In the farmyard to the west are the ruins of a Norman chapel. Today the Brockhampton Estate, some 2,000 acres which includes both the manor and chapel, belongs to the National Trust.

▲ Kenilworth Castle, Warwickshire

After the Norman Conquest, Kenilworth belonged to the Crown and was part of the royal manor of Stoneleigh. Early in the twelfth century Henry I granted the estate to his chamberlain and treasurer, Geoffrey de Clinton, who divided it into two portions: the part downstream of the Finham Brook he donated, for the foundation of an Augustinian monastery; the part upstream he reserved for a castle for himself, with its attendant park and chase. The first castle, built of timber and earth, was sited on a knoll of rock and gravel and protected on all sides by marshland. In the latter half of the twelfth century the defences were rebuilt in stone and extensively improved during the reign of King John (1199–1216). Further alterations and additions, notably in the fourteenth and sixteenth centuries, transformed the castle into a palace. In 1649, at the end of the Civil War, Parliament ordered the castle's demolition. Although the vast defensive lake was drained, the stronghold was only partially demolished.

▶ Warwick Castle and River Avon, Warwickshire

Occupying a sandstone cliff rising sheer from the River Avon, Warwick Castle dates from 914, when Ethelfleda, the 'Lady of the Mercians' and daughter of Alfred the Great, fortified the site against marauding Danes. After the Norman Conquest the Anglo-Saxon stronghold was replaced by a wooden motte-and-bailey castle, which, in turn, was replaced in the twelfth and thirteenth centuries by a fortress of stone. Guy's Tower and Caesar's tower, however, were built in the fourteenth century. During the Middle Ages Warwick was by far the most famous of all the Midland castles. Its powerful earls have featured prominently in many events in the nation's history, including the trial and execution of Piers Gaveston, Edward II's favourite, and the struggle for the crown between the rival dynasties of Lancaster and York. During the Civil War the castle was saved from destruction by the Parliamentarians because of Robert Greville's support for their cause. Today the castle, owned by Madame Tussaud's, is one of England's most popular tourist attractions.

▶ Snowscene, near Wilmcote, Warwickshire

The ancient Forest of Arden lay to the north of the River Avon in Warwickshire. Although it has long been cleared, small isolated patches of woodland still survive. In addition, timber from the forest has been preserved in many of the older buildings, including Mary Arden's House at Wilmcote, three miles north-west of Stratford-upon-Avon. In the mid-sixteenth century the Tudor farmstead was called 'Ashbyes' and belonged to Robert Arden, a prosperous yeoman farmer, who owned land not only at Wilmcote but also at Snitterfield. Today the property, named after his daughter Mary (Shakespeare's mother) belongs to the Shakespeare Birthplace Trust. Dating from the early sixteenth century, the oak-timbered farmhouse stands on a substantial foundation of locally quarried blue-grey stone, while its roof is covered with hand-made clay tiles. The barns and outbuildings at the rear of the house contain a fascinating collection of old farming implements and tools. These, linked to the adjacent buildings of Glebe Farm, form the Shakespeare Countryside Museum.

◄ Chesterton Windmill, Windmill Hill, Warwickshire

The manor house of the Peyto family was erected in about 1650-60, and demolished in about 1802. But the windmill was originally built in 1632 for Sir Edward Peyto and reputedly designed by Inigo Jones. Now in the care of Warwickshire County Council, it is occasionally open to the public. Chesterton Windmill was described by William Field in his *History of*

Warwick and Leamington, published in 1815:

'Without the fliers, the mill, which is of a circular form, would resemble a large temple, of no graceful symmetry. The body is supported by six arches, with pilaster capitals; and beneath them, by ordinary wooden stairs, is the ascent to the interior. The mill is surmounted by a leaden dome, which revolves for the purpose of shifting the fliers affixed to it, as the state of the wind requires.'

▲ Anne Hathaway's Cottage, Shottery, Warwickshire

Anne Hathaway, the daughter of Richard Hathaway, a yeoman farmer, was born in 1556 at Shottery – a small hamlet on the fringe of the Forest of Arden, a mile to the west of Stratford-upon-Avon. Originally a spacious twelve-roomed farmhouse, known as 'Hewlands', the property in which she lived is now popularly referred to as 'Anne Hathaway's Cottage'. The oldest part of the building, with its stone foundations, timber-framed walls (mainly infilled with wattle and daub),

tiny latticed windows, tall brick chimney stacks and high-pitched thatched roof, dates from the fifteenth century. It was owned and occupied by the descendants of the Hathaway family until 1892, when it was purchased by the Shakespeare Birthplace Trust, who have furnished the rooms much as they would have been in Anne's time. Before their marriage in 1582, William Shakespeare would have been a regular visitor. Perhaps the courting couple sat together – under the watchful eyes of her parents – on the old oak settle now in the living room.

▶ Toy Cottage, Church Lench, Worcestershire

In the folds of the farmed and orchard-cloaked hills north of Evesham are a number of black and white villages and hamlets known collectively as 'The Lenches' (named after the Lench family who once owned much land in the area). The largest, Church Lench, once belonged to the abbey of Evesham. Its church, dedicated to All Saints, dates from Norman times, although the tower was only completed in the sixteenth century. Rous Lench is named after the Rous family, who acquired the estate towards the end of the reign of Richard II (1377–99). Rous Lench Court, an early Tudor house, was owned by the Reverend W.K.W. Chafy between 1876 and 1916. As lord of the manor, he built the unusual pillar box

by the village green. Standing on a stone plinth and bearing the Chafy coat of arms, the timber-framed structure resembles a miniature gabled house. A similar box can be found at nearby Radford. In addition to the two Lenches mentioned there is also Atch Lench, Ab (or Abbots) Lench and Sheriffs Lench, and Lenchwick too.

▶ Malvern Priory, Great Malvern, Worcestershire

The Malvern Hills rise from the fertile plain of the River Severn to form a narrow, north-south ridge of granite and gneiss some nine miles long. Worcestershire Beacon is the highest point, reaching 1,395 feet above sea level; from the summit there are extensive views over much of Middle England. On the eastern slopes lie the 'Seven Sisters': six villages – Little Malvern, Malvern Wells, The Wyche (or South Malvern), Malvern Link, North Malvern and West Malvern – and one town – Great Malvern. Malvern Wells and Great Malvern became celebrated spas, prospering on the medicinal

properties of the local spring water. The priory at Great Malvern was founded for Benedictine monks in 1085 by Aldwyn, a hermit, with the encouragement of St Wulfstan, the last Saxon Bishop of Worcester. At Little Malvern are the remains of a second, smaller Benedictine priory. Nearby, in the cemetery of the Roman Catholic church of St Wulstan (sic), the composer Edward Elgar (1857–1934) lies buried.

▶ Hidcote Bartrim, Gloucestershire

On the western slopes of Ilmington Downs, four miles north-east of Chipping Campden, Hidcote Bartrim contains one of the most celebrated gardens in England – Hidcote Manor Garden – created by Lawrence Waterbury Johnston in the early twentieth century. Originally a wild, windswept area of uncultivated farmland, consisting of a few specimen trees and a late seventeenth-century manor house with its attendant thatched cottages, Hidcote was transformed, not into a single large garden covering some ten acres, but into a series of small gardens separated by hedges: the White Garden, the Stilt Garden, the Old Garden, the Terrace Garden with its gazebo, Mrs Winthrop's Garden, with its pair of Hardy Chusan Palms, the Long Walk, the Bathing Pool Garden and many more. The property is now in the care of the National Trust. Just beyond the manor house is the hamlet of Hidcote Bartrim, with its thatched stone cottages, duck pond, well and farm. Its main street, no wider than a narrow lane, ends in open fields which produce a variety of crops from strawberries to potatoes.

▶ Chipping Campden, from The Mile Drive, near Dover's Hill, Gloucestershire

Chipping Campden's prosperity as an important centre of the medieval wool trade is not only reflected in the great Perpendicular 'wool' church of St James, but in many of the houses that line the town's wide and curving main street. The Market Hall was built in 1627 by Sir Baptist Hicks, who also built the terrace of almshouses leading to the church and, opposite, a magnificent Jacobean mansion. All that now remains of the latter, destroyed by fire during the Civil War, are the lodges and gateway. Perhaps the town's greatest benefactor was William Grevel, according to the Latin inscription on his large brass in the church, 'formerly a citizen of London and flower of the wool merchants of all England, who died on the first day of October Anno Domini 1401'. His house, built in the late fourteenth century, still stands in the High Street. To the north-west of the town is Dover's Hill, named after Robert Dover, who founded the 'Cotswold Olimpick Games' (a unique form of entertainment which involved such events as horse-racing, dancing and shin-kicking) in about 1612.

▲ Bury End, near Broadway, Gloucestershire

From Broadway, that 'show-piece' of Cotswold villages, the road heads south past Bury End to hug the eastern slopes of a deep coombe, becoming steeper as it approaches the high wolds beyond the upland village of Snowshill. The waters which rise at the head of the coombe flow north-westward into the Vale of Evesham where they join the Badsey Brook, a tributary of the River Avon. To the west of the coombe, a long wooded crest marks the top of the Cotswold escarpment, dropping abruptly to the villages of Buckland, Laverton and Stanton beyond. In winter the roads are often impassable, with snow blowing down from the open wolds to create deep drifts, that effectively cut off the villages and farmsteads. The long distance Cotswold Way, following an ancient track from Broadway, climbs up over the brow of Burhill, where there are the remains of a prehistoric settlement, and continues along the wooded ridge towards Winchcombe and Cleeve Hill.

▶ Broadway Beacon, near Broadway, Worcestershire

At 1,024 feet above sea level, Broadway Hill is the second highest point in the Cotswolds, offering extensive views across the Vale of Evesham towards Wales. It is said that the wife of the 6th Earl of Coventry wanted to know whether the summit – traditionally used as a beacon site – was visible from his family seat at Croome Court, some fifteen miles to the north-west. The Earl arranged for a bonfire to be lit on the hill and, realizing that it could be seen, ordered a tower to be built on the spot. The folly was designed right at the end of the eighteenth century by James Wyatt. Today the structure, some sixty-five feet high, is part of the Broadway Tower Country Park and contains a number of exhibitions, including one on the history of Cotswold wool, and another on social reformer, artist, craftsman, poet and designer William Morris (1834–96), who was a frequent guest at the tower, along with Dante Gabriel Rossetti (1828–82) and Edward Burne-Jones (1833–98).

▲ Snowshill, Gloucestershire

Nestling beneath the brow of Oat Hill, high in the wolds south of Broadway, the remote village of Snowshill clusters around a triangular dry-stone-walled green in the middle of which stands the parish church. The Cotswold stone cottages, set at different angles and levels into the hillside, are steeply roofed in the vernacular style, having porous limestone slates which decrease in size from the eaves to the ridge. The church of St Barnabas, completely rebuilt in 1864, stands on the site of an earlier foundation traditionally thought to have been dedicated to St George. Snowshill once belonged to Kenulf (or Coenwulf), King of Mercia, who gave the 840-acre estate to Winchcombe Abbey in the early ninth century. It was one of a number of upland manors where the abbey's huge flocks were allowed to graze before being driven down into the valleys to be washed and sheared. Snowshill Manor dates from about 1500 and contains the astonishing collection of bygones accumulated by Charles Paget Wade, a wealthy eccentric who died in 1956.

▲ Compton Wynyates, near Brailes, Warwickshire

Situated in a deep wooded hollow, Compton Wynyates was considered by Pevsner to be 'the most perfect picture-book house of the Early Tudor decades, the most perfect in England in the specific picturesque' (Buildings of England: Warwickshire). The estate has belonged to the Compton family since the early thirteenth century and even today is owned by one of their descendants, the 7th Marquess of Northampton. During the Civil War the house was captured by the Parliamentarians, and was only returned to the Comptons after a heavy fine had been paid and an order had been issued by Parliament to fill in the moat and demolish the battlements. In the latter half of the eighteenth century, after much of the family fortune had been lost through gambling and reckless extravagance, Lord Northampton gave instructions for the house to be demolished. His agent, fortunately, did little more than brick up the windows to avoid window tax. Although many old guide books wax lyrical about the topiary garden, it no longer exists.

▶ The Bodleian Library, Radcliffe Camera and St Mary's Church, Oxford, Oxfordshire

'That sweet city with her dreaming spires', as Matthew Arnold called Oxford, stands on the site of a crossing-place of the rivers Cherwell and Thames (locally called the Isis). The evolution of the market town into a university city – the first in England – began in the eleventh century, possibly stimulated by the expulsion of English scholars from Paris in 1167. Although University College, founded in 1249, is the earliest surviving college, it was Merton, founded in 1249, which set the pattern adopted as the standard by many later foundations. The Bodleian Library, founded by Thomas Bodley, was officially opened in 1602. Now part of the Bodleian, the domed Radcliffe Camera was built in 1737-49 as an independent library by James Gibbs, with money bequeathed by the eminent physician Dr John Radcliffe. From the elegantly spired tower of the university church of St Mary the Virgin, built between 1315 and 1325, there are splendid views over the city. The photograph was taken from the Sheldonian Theatre, designed by Christopher Wren in 1663–9.

▶ Great Tew, Oxfordshire

Set in a hollow of low, tree-embowered hills, the village of Great Tew owes much of its present charm to the landscaping skills of John Claudius Loudon, the Scottish architect and agriculturalist, who managed the estate for Colonel George Stratton at the beginning of the nineteenth century. Many of the cottages – some thatched, others roofed with stone tiles and built in the traditional Cotswold style, with mullioned windows, drip mouldings and moulded door frames – were erected by Lucius Cary, 2nd Viscount Falkland, Secretary of State to Charles I, who was killed at the battle of Newbury in 1643. The Falkland Arms, beside the village green, is named after him. His mansion, long demolished, stood in the park beside the church of St Michael and All Angels. Matthew Robinson Boulton – the son of Matthew Boulton, considered by some to be the 'Father of the Industrial Revolution' – purchased the estate from Stratton in 1815. In addition to erecting more properties, he embellished many of the existing cottages with porches and other rustic features.

◄ Vale of the White Horse, from Whitehorse Hill, Oxfordshire

The Vale of the White Horse takes its name from a strange, beak-headed animal cut into the turf escarpment of Whitehorse Hill, the summit of which is crowned by the Iron Age hillfort of Uffington Castle. Measuring some 360 feet in length and 130 feet in height, it is the earliest and most famous white horse hill-figure in England. Unlike most other white horses, it faces right. Although its purpose is unknown, experts suggest that it may have been the emblem of the Atrebates, a tribe from Belgic Gaul (northern France) who occupied the hillfort in the first century BC. An optical dating technique, however, pioneered by Oxford University archaeologists, has shown that the animal was first constructed in the late Bronze Age, some 3,000 years ago. The flat-topped mound of Dragon Hill, below the horse, is said to be the spot where St George killed the dragon. In a grove of trees, to the south-west, there is a Neolithic burial site known as Wayland's Smithy. The site is unusual in that the tomb has been built on top of an even older barrow.

▲ Goodrich Castle, Herefordshire

Standing on a high cliff overlooking the valley of the River Wye, the red sandstone castle at Goodrich was first recorded in a document of c. 1101. Known as 'Godric's Castle' (almost certainly after Godric of Mappestone who held nearby Howle during the Domesday survey of 1086), it was strategically sited to protect an ancient ford across the river. Originally built of earth and timber, the fortress was rebuilt in stone during the mid-twelfth century. Further rebuilding in the late thirteenth century by the powerful Earls of Pembroke, however, demolished much of the Norman stronghold, but retained its square three-storeyed keep. In 1326 the castle was seized by Richard Talbot, whose descendants (created Earls of Shrewsbury in the fifteenth century) made it their principal residence for many years. Occupied by both Parliamentarians and Royalists during the Civil War, the castle was partially demolished after the surrender of Charles I in 1646.

▶ Wicken Fen, Wicken, Cambridgeshire

Britain's oldest nature reserve and one of the few surviving remnants of undrained fenland in East Anglia, Wicken Fen (733 acres) is owned and managed by the National Trust. Sedge Fen, the area nearest the village of Wicken, has never been drained (causing the peat to shrink and the land to sink), and stands islanded several feet above an intensively cultivated sea of sunken farmland. A small wooden smock-drainage mill helps to maintain water levels, pumping water in to protect the spongy wetland from drying out. Boundary banks also help. Without careful management, the fenland would gradually be taken over by scrubland, eventually becoming oak and ash woodland. Fen Cottage, built in traditional fenland materials, is furnished in 1930s style.

With its network of rivers and drainage channels, stretches of coastal marshland, and wetland expanses of fens and broads, the East of England is one of the most watery landscapes in the country, though it records the lowest level of annual rainfall. After the Ice Age much of the region was flooded, especially in the vicinity of the Wash, where many Midland rivers enter the North Sea. The gradual accumulation of silt and sand caused land levels to rise and plants to take root, whilst changes in climate and fluctuations in water levels slowly transformed the decaying vegetation into peat – the essence of the Fenland landscape.

Covering some 1,500 square miles of Cambridgeshire, Norfolk and Lincolnshire, the Fens have two distinct parts: the silt-lands around and bordering the Wash; and the peat-lands, or 'Black Fens', which lie further inland. The islands of high, firm ground that stood out above the surrounding marshlands were settled during prehistoric times. Drainage in the seventeenth and eighteenth centuries turned the Fens into one of the richest arable areas in the country. Today very few tracts of primordial fenland remain.

The Broads are not only England's largest stretch of wetlands and the refuge of many endangered species of wildlife and plants, they are also a mecca for many thousands of holiday-makers, the majority of whom are boating or sailing enthusiasts, attracted by some 125 miles of lock-free navigable waterways. Fed by six principal rivers, the broads – or lakes – are the remains of shallow peat diggings, created in medieval times and later flooded. The unique wetland area, covering an area of some 117 square miles and containing forty or so broads, became Britain's eleventh National Park in 1989.

Despite being a largely man-made landscape, the region contains much that epitomises the traditional English scene. It is not surprising, then, that one of the country's greatest landscape painters, John Constable, was born in Suffolk, finding his main inspiration in the scenes of his childhood around East Bergholt and the Stour valley. 'Painting is another word for feeling,' he wrote in 1823. Strangely, in this largely uncluttered land of ever-changing lights, infinite horizons and limitless skies, 'feeling' finds fresh and inspirational relevance.

▼ Lavender Field, near Heacham, Norfolk

Said to have been introduced into Britain from the Mediterranean by the Romans who were aware of its healing, soothing and insect-repellent properties, lavender is now commonly grown for its fragrant flowers and aromatic foliage. Despite being a favourite in gardens throughout the country, the only place in England where the plant is grown commercially on a large scale is at Caley Mill, Heacham. Built of local carstone in the 1820s, the water mill was originally used to grind corn. In 1935, when it was purchased by Francis 'Ginger' Dusgate of nearby Fring Hall, the mill was in a dilapidated condition. Restoration of the property began in 1954 and today, with alterations and extensions, it is the headquarters of Norfolk Lavender. The company, incorporated in 1941, was founded by the nurseryman Linn Chilvers, who went into partnership with Dusgate in 1932 to grow and distil lavender: the former providing 13,000 plants and the latter six acres of land. The lavender flowers were harvested by hand, using small sickle-shaped knives, until 1964, when the first mechanical cutter was introduced.

▶ Cliffs at Hunstanton, Norfolk

Although only sixty feet high, the cliffs at Hunstanton are famous for their horizontally striped Cretaceous beds, made of successive layers of gingerbread-coloured carstone and red and white chalk. Because cataclysmic movements of the earth's crust caused the sedimentary layers to tilt or slope from west to east in Norfolk, the white chalk forms the top of the cliffs at Hunstanton and the base of those at Weybourne, while at Great Yarmouth it lies some 500 feet below sea level. New Hunstanton – developed after the arrival of the railway in 1862 – is unusual in that it is the only seaside resort in East Anglia to face west, thereby providing both visitors and residents with a view of the sun setting over the Wash. The ancient track of the Peddar's Way starts in Suffolk and ends at Holme-Next-the-Sea, some

two miles north-east of Old Hunstanton. Although it has no obvious finishing point, apart from the sea, it has been suggested that the path was part of a route north into Lincolnshire that crossed the Wash by a ferry.

**◄ Thornham Channel,
Thornham, Norfolk**

Situated by a tidal creek amidst extensive saltmarshes and shifting mud flats, the once-flourishing natural harbour at Thornham is so silted up that it can only be used by small boats, while the village, which originally stood at the edge of the sea, is now almost a mile inland. Built mostly of local flint and pink and white chalk, the village contains three inns, the oldest – the Lifeboat – dating from the late sixteenth century, when it was a farmhouse. Aerial photographs taken in 1948 revealed the remains of a small Iron Age fort, south-west of the village. Victims of the Black Death, which struck Thornham in 1348, bringing the rebuilding of the church to an abrupt halt, were buried near the harbour in the Plague Pits, now more tastefully known as the Plug Pits. In the partly Early English, partly Perpendicular church of All Saints is a scale model of the windmill which once stood on the brick base tower opposite the Pits. Originally a post mill standing on Beacon Hill to the south of the village, it was dismantled, moved and re-erected (without the post) on the base in about 1880, thereby becoming a 'composite' mill.

▼ Fishing Boats at Brancaster Staithe, Norfolk

Largely consisting of low-lying marshland, broken by ever-changing sand and mud flats, dunes, spits and shingle ridges, the thirty-three miles of Norfolk coast between Hunstanton and Sheringham has remained relatively unspoilt by twentieth-century developments. Nevertheless, parts of the tidal saltmarsh have been drained and converted to grazing land, while some of the sand dunes cover artificial embankments. Within the area are twelve nature reserves, probably the best known being Scolt Head island and Blakeney Point. Over the centuries most of the old ports along this part of the coast declined because their harbours, or havens, silted up. During Roman times, for example, the main channels at Brancaster were navigable to wharves near Branodunum. Today, the few traces of the fort that remain are separated from the sea by a wide expanse of saltmarsh. Brancaster Staithe, opposite Scolt Head island, is a popular yachting centre. 'Staithe' is derived from the Old English for 'landing place'.

▼ Church of St. Mary the Virgin, Titchwell, Norfolk

One of a number of villages strung out along the north Norfolk coast, Titchwell is an ancient settlement dating back to Anglo-Saxon times. Like many of its buildings, the church – mentioned in the Domesday survey of 1086 – is built of flint; the cheapest and most abundant material available in the locality. The bell tower, topped with a little lead spike, is round because it is easier to create a circular shape with flint than one with corners. A similar round tower, dating from the

Anglo-Saxon period, can be found further east along the coast at Burnham Deepdale, one of seven villages in the area that take the first part of their name from the little River Burn (the others being Burnham Norton, Burnham Overy, Burnham Thorpe, Burnham Sutton, Burnham Ulph and Burnham Westgate – the latter three now form Burnham Market). Lord Horatio Nelson was born in the old parsonage (now demolished) at Burnham Thorpe on 29 September 1758. The church of All Saints where he was christened stands over half a mile away to the north.

▲ Cley-Next-the-Sea, Norfolk

Overlooking Blakeney Harbour, the River Glaven and the Cley Marshes nature reserve, the brick tower windmill at Cley-Next-the-Sea was built in the early eighteenth century. It ceased working in about 1912, and has now been converted into a guest house. In the medieval period, when the River Glaven was navigable as far inland as Glandford, Cley, Wiveton and Blakeney were thriving ports (known as the Glaven ports), mainly exporting wool, grain and fish to the Low Countries. The ports of Cley and Wiveton were both centred around their respective churches, which faced each other across a wide expanse of tidal water. However, in the early seventeenth century, due to the construction of flood-protection and land-reclamation banks, the river began to silt up, thereby preventing ships from reaching Cley. The construction of a new quay in deeper water nearer the sea (with its attendant wharves, warehouses and granaries), together with the destruction of much of the old town by the great fire of 1612, had the effect of moving the centre of Cley north, to the area where the windmill now stands.

◄ St Benet's Level Windpump, Thurne, The Broads, Norfolk

The two restored drainage mills near the Broadland village of Thurne are of the brick tower type, with white caps and sails. Standing on opposite banks of the River Thurne, the red-brick St Benet's Level mill (not open to the public) is known locally as 'Jenny', while the white-painted Thurne Dyke windpump (containing a small exhibition of Broadland windpumps) is known as 'Jack'. To the west of Thurne, on the north bank of the Bure, are the lonely remains of St Benet's Abbey, first founded in the ninth century and refounded by King Canute in about 1020. In the eighteenth century a brick tower windpump (now derelict) was erected in the ruins of the monastic gatehouse. The records of the monastery helped provide conclusive evidence that the Broads were not formed naturally, but were created artificially by the removal of massive quantities of peat for fuel during medieval times. The pits, excavated to depths ranging from five to fifteen feet, were flooded by the end of the fourteenth century due to gradually rising water levels.

▲ Castle Acre Priory, near Swaffham, Norfolk

As a reward for his part in the Norman Conquest, William de Warenne, one of William I's most powerful and trusted supporters, was granted lands in over a dozen English counties. Although his main seat was at Lewes in Sussex, Warenne made Castle Acre – situated astride the ancient Peddar's Way near where it crosses the River Nar – the centre of his Norfolk estates. The first castle, resembling a 'country house', was built on the hill-top site of an earlier fortification, possibly dating back to prehistoric times. It was transformed into a mighty keep during the twelfth century and the defences surrounding it were strengthened greatly. The first Cluniac priory, probably founded by Warenne's son, the 2nd Earl of Surrey, in c. 1090, lay within the castle precincts, but was soon moved south-west of the town, to the low-lying valley of the Nar. Established as a daughter house of St Pancras at Lewes, the priory was surrendered to Henry VIII in 1537 and now, like the castle, the ruins are in the care of English Heritage.

◀ **Ely Cathedral, from Castle Mound, Cambridgeshire**

Before the draining of the Fens in the seventeenth and eighteenth centuries, the small city of Ely stood on an island surrounded by marshland. Built between 1083 and 1189, the cathedral still dominates the flat Fenland landscape for miles around. It stands on the site of a monastery founded in the seventh century by Etheldreda, daughter of Anna, King of the East Angles, and Queen of Northumbria. Destroyed by marauding Danes in 869, the monastery was refounded as a Benedictine abbey in 970 and in 1109 the church became a cathedral. During the thirteenth century the cathedral was extended, while in 1322 the Norman central tower collapsed, destroying parts of the choir, nave and transepts. The tower was replaced by a unique Octagon, supported by eight stone columns and crowned by a timber lantern, the whole structure weighing some 400 tons. Seeming to hang in space, it is an incredible feat of construction and an architectural gem. The fourteenth-century Lady Chapel, attached to a corner of the north transept, is the largest chapel of its kind in England.

▲ **Denver Mill, near Downham Market, Norfolk**

Of the 6,000 or so watermills recorded in the Domesday survey of 1086, some 500 were in Norfolk. During the century that followed, however, windmills were introduced into the country, possibly by returning crusaders who had seen them in the Middle East. Because they could be built on almost any exposed site (and despite being less reliable), they soon outnumbered watermills, especially in East Anglia, where they still remain a traditional feature of the landscape. The six-storeyed tower mill at Denver, built in 1835, has an ogee cap more typical of Lincolnshire mills than of those in Norfolk, which tend to resemble an upturned clinker-built boat. Converted to diesel power in 1941, it ceased to operate in 1969 after the death of the last miller. Although the majority of windmills were built to grind corn, a large number of those around the Fens and Broads were designed to drain the marshland by pumping or lifting the water into rivers and dykes which then carried it directly to the sea. Today, wind power is not only used for milling and drainage but as an environmentally clean method of generating electricity.

▲ Houghton Mill, near Huntingdon, Cambridgeshire

In 1086, when the Domesday survey was compiled, there were over twenty watermills in Huntingdonshire, all powered by the River Great Ouse or its tributaries. The present mill at Houghton, standing on an artificial island on the Ouse, dates from the seventeenth century, and is one of the last to survive along the river. Owned by the National Trust, the large five-storeyed brick and timber building, with tarred weatherboarding and slate roof (originally thatched), contains much of its nineteenth-century machinery, including ten pairs of millstones. Although its three water wheels were removed and replaced by sluices in the 1930s, the partly restored machinery (now operated by electricity) continues to grind corn into flour. During the seventeenth century the Ouse was made navigable for some seventy-five miles from the Wash, near King's Lynn, to Bedford. In the water meadows around Houghton the river divides into a series of interconnected channels, the northernmost of which is occupied by the mill.

► King's and Clare Colleges, Cambridge, Cambridgeshire

Long before it became internationally famous as a university city, Cambridge was a thriving Fenland market town and busy inland port. Linked to the Wash and the sea by way of the Cam and Great Ouse, its origins date back at least to Roman times, when there was a small town with a bridge over the Cam (or Granta). Although a school of learning may already have been in existence, the university is traditionally said to owe its origin to a disturbance at Oxford in 1209, which caused many teachers and scholars to migrate to Cambridge. The oldest college, Peterhouse, was founded in 1284. It was not until 1869, however, that the first women's college was founded (at Girton, some two miles north of the city); and it was not until 1948 that women finally achieved equal university status with men. From left to right in the photograph are: Clare College, first founded in 1326 as University

Hall and rebuilt between 1638 and 1719; King's College Chapel, begun by Henry VI in 1446 and completed in 1515; and King's College Fellows' Building, designed by James Gibbs in 1724.

▼ Bridge & Chapel of St Leger, St Ives, Cambridgeshire

Spanning the Great Ouse at the old market town and inland port of St Ives is a stone-built, six-arched bridge, dating from the early fifteenth century

and noted for supporting a rare bridge-chapel. The medieval name of the town is derived from St Ivo, a Persian bishop who, according to legend, became a hermit in Huntingdonshire during the fifth or sixth century. Little remains of the Benedictine priory, founded during the Anglo-Saxon period as a cell of Ramsey Abbey. At its dissolution in 1539, because it was a small and relatively poor house, it is possible that the prior was the only monk in residence. Records show that he received a pension of twelve pounds a year, and was allowed to reside in the bridge-chapel. Dominating the marketplace is a bronze statue of Oliver Cromwell, who lived and farmed in the area for several years. Born at Huntingdon in 1599, he ruled England as Lord Protector from 1653 until his death in 1658. Not surprisingly, the area around Huntingdon, St Ives and the Great Ouse is known as 'Cromwell Country'.

▲ St Mary's Church & 'Hyde Park Corner Cottages', Cavendish, Suffolk

With its broad green-, and pink-washed thatched almshouses nestling beneath the fourteenth-century tower of St Mary's church, Cavendish is one of the most photographed villages in East Anglia. Situated on the north bank of the upper Ouse, some three miles downstream from the small wool town of Clare, the village was once the main home of the Cavendish family (now the Dukes of Devonshire). Sir John Cavendish, Chief Justice of the King's Bench, was beheaded in 1381 at Bury St Edmunds by supporters of Wat Tyler, who sought revenge for the killing of their leader by his son. In his will he left sufficient money to rebuild the chancel of Cavendish church. The Old Rectory, originally a timber-framed farmhouse, is now the headquarters of the Sue Ryder Foundation, an international charity formed in 1953 by Sue Ryder (later Lady Ryder of Warsaw) to care for the sick and disabled. The almshouses, known as 'Hyde Park Corner Cottages', date from the fourteenth century, but have been much restored.

▶ Church Street, Lavenham, Suffolk

Almost every street in the medieval wool town of Lavenham is lined with timber-framed houses, many of which have overhanging jetties, and are so twisted and warped with age that they appear to be in imminent danger of collapse. After the 1330s, when Flemish weavers were encouraged to settle in England by Edward III, Lavenham developed as a cloth-making centre, famous throughout much of Europe for its blue cloth. The growing prosperity of the market town in the fifteenth century is reflected in many of its buildings, particularly in the magnificent 'wool' church of St Peter and St Paul. Its knapped flint tower, erected between 1486 and 1525, is 141 feet high and dominates not only the town but the whole countryside around. In the late seventeenth century many of the half-timbered houses and cottages were plastered over and, in places, decoration was added in the form of pargeting. In the mid-eighteenth century some of the properties had their overhangs and timber fronts hidden behind a facade of Georgian brick.

◀ Moot Hall, Aldeburgh, Suffolk

The little seaside town of Aldeburgh on the Suffolk coast is famous for being the birthplace of the poet George Crabbe (1754–1832), and the home of the composer Benjamin Britten (1913–76). One of the tales in Crabbe's poem 'The Borough' (1810), based on Aldeburgh, inspired Britten's opera Peter Grimes (1945). The annual music festival, co-founded by Britten in 1948, is held in the resort each June. Since 1967, however, the major performances have been in the Maltings concert hall, some five miles inland at Snape. The Moot Hall, housing a museum of the town's maritime history, was built in the sixteenth century when Aldeburgh was a fishing and ship-building port of some importance. The half-timbered building was originally in the centre of the town, but coastal erosion means that now it stands almost on the shingle beach. The Martello Tower, just south of Aldeburgh, was the northernmost link in the chain of defences against possible French invasion that stretched around the coast to Seaford in Sussex. Built between 1805 and 1812, it has now been converted into a dwelling.

THE EAST

▶ Mistley Towers, Essex

Overlooking the widening estuary of the River Stour are two striking neo-classical church towers designed by the architect Robert Adam in 1776. They originally stood at the east and west ends of the church of St Mary, built earlier in the same century. When the building was demolished in 1870 the towers were saved, the intention being that they might be used as mausoleums. Representing a rare example of an ecclesiastical work by Adam, the towers are now in the care of English Heritage. Although Golding Constable, a prosperous corn merchant, had a wharf at the river port of Mistley in the eighteenth century, his main business was centred on Flatford Mill, some three miles upstream. His fourth child, John, was born nearby at East Bergholt in 1776. Instead of joining his father's firm as was expected, he devoted himself to painting, finding inspiration in the English landscape, especially the scenes of his childhood around the lower Stour valley (known even in his lifetime as 'Constable Country').

▶ Orford Castle, Suffolk

Commissioned by Henry II as a royal stronghold and coastal defence, Orford Castle is noted for the unusual design of its keep, and for the fact that it is the earliest castle in Britain for which there are detailed records of construction and costs. Begun in 1165 and completed in 1173, the castle occupies a previously unfortified site and was built with exceptional speed. For example, it seems that the massive ninety-foot-high keep (all that now survives of the castle above ground) was finished in just two years (1165–7). Instead of the characteristic great rectangular tower of the period, the external walls of the keep are polygonal in plan, with three huge rectangular turrets serving as buttresses. According to the medieval chronicler Ralph of Coggeshall, a naked man-like creature with a long, shaggy beard, was caught in the nets of local fishermen and handed over to the first constable of the castle, Bartholomew de Glanville. Known as the Wild Man of Orford, the 'merman' eventually escaped from his guards and fled back to the sea, never to be seen again

▶ St Andrew's Church, Greensted, Essex

The timbers of St Andrew's at Greensted, near Chipping Ongar, have been scientifically dated to reveal that the Anglo-Saxon building was constructed in about AD 850, making it the oldest wooden church in the world. Standing on the site of a seventh-century foundation, and possibly an even earlier pagan place of worship, the church has been considerably altered and extended over the centuries. The nave – its walls built of oak logs split in half and positioned vertically, with the rounded sides on the outside – originally had a thatched, windowless roof. It was tiled and given three dormer windows in about 1500, at the same time that the south porch was added and the chancel rebuilt in brick. The wooden tower, with its shingled broach spire, dates from the seventeenth century, maybe earlier, and is weatherboarded in typical Essex style. Extensive restoration in Victorian times included shortening the ancient timbers of the nave walls because of decay, and footing them on a base of brick.

▶ **Cuckmere Valley, from Cradle Hill, East Sussex**

From its source in the heart of the Sussex Weald, the Cuckmere River flows southward for some seventeen miles to enter the English Channel at Cuckmere Haven. Between Alfriston and the sea it meanders dramatically, but a bypass – a straight artificial channel – was cut downstream from Exceat in 1846. Although the river was once navigable as far inland as Alfriston, it never had a port at its mouth. The flat, pebble beach at Cuckmere Haven, however, was once popular with smugglers for landing their contraband. The photograph was taken looking east towards Charleston Bottom and the dark woods of Friston Forest.

Since prehistoric times, when Britain became an island, successive waves of immigrants and invaders from different parts of Europe have crossed the Channel to enter the country through the south-east, the 'Gateway to England'. All have left their mark on the landscape and scenery of the region, whether by simply helping to clear the almost impenetrable forest of Andreadsweald or by contributing to the construction of innumerable fortifications around the coast.

Although William the Conqueror founded many castles and monasteries, including Battle Abbey, he also created a royal hunting preserve in Hampshire, calling it Nova Foresta, or 'New Forest'. Today most of the forest, which covers an area of some 145 square miles, is managed by the Forestry Commission on behalf of the Crown. It was given the unofficial status of a National Park in 1992. The main upland areas of the region are the rolling chalk ridges of the North and South Downs, where evidence of prehistoric occupation can be found. Together with the Hampshire Downs, they form a horseshoe around the Kent and Sussex Weald, terminating abruptly when they meet the sea to form the famous white cliffs of Dover and Beachy Head, respectively. In the Weald, where only remnants of the once-dense forest of Andreadsweald remain, high ridges of sandstone alternate with valleys, or troughs, of softer clays to create a landscape ideal for growing hops and fruit. Because of the rich fertility of the Wealden countryside, Kent is traditionally known as the 'Garden of England'.

Because of its proximity to mainland Europe, the south-east has always been vulnerable to invasion – hence the heavily fortified coastline. The last attempted invasion was made over the skies of the region during the Battle of Britain in 1940. The completion of the thirty-one-mile Chunnel, or Eurotunnel, heralded the start of a new, and far more peaceful invasion of England. The opening of the Channel Tunnel in 1994 confirmed the region's status as the 'Gateway to England'. For the first time in some 7,000 years it became possible to cross the Channel on dry land, an achievement no less significant than Louis Blériot's historic flight across the Strait of Dover in 1909. For those who wish to celebrate the unique and treasured heritage of south-east England's past, there could be no better introduction than to enter the country through one of the greatest engineering feats of modern times.

▲ River Thames and St Paul's Cathedral, from Waterloo Bridge, London

By the third century, the settlement of Londinium had become the capital of Roman Britain and the sixth largest city in the empire. Covering 330 acres with the entire south side a waterfront, London remained more or less confined within the limits of its Roman walls until the sixteenth century. During medieval times the capital was a divided city with two centres of authority: the area within the walls (still known as the City of London) came under the control of the powerful merchant guilds; while Westminster (some two miles upstream) was subject to the rule of the king, and later to that of parliament. St Paul's Cathedral is celebrated as an outstanding example of English Baroque and the finest of Christopher Wren's works. Built between 1675 and 1710, it stands in the City on the site of four previous foundations, the earliest dating from 604. All were burnt down, and the last, Old St Paul's, was destroyed in the Great Fire of London in 1666. The crypt, in which Wren lies buried, is the largest in Europe. His epitaph, translated from the Latin, reads: 'If you seek his monument, look about you.'

◄ **Houses of Parliament and River Thames, from the Embankment, London**

The first monarch to build a palace at Westminster was Edward the Confessor (King of England from 1042 to 1066), who also built the abbey beside it. The present Westminster Abbey dates mainly from the thirteenth and fourteenth centuries, while the two western towers were added in the eighteenth century. Westminster Palace, the main residence of the monarchs until Henry VIII moved his court to Whitehall, was destroyed by fire in 1834. The magnificent hall, however, built by William II, survived and was incorporated into the present Houses of Parliament (or New Palace of Westminster). Built between 1837 and 1868 in the Gothic Revival style by Charles Barry (with the assistance of Augustus Pugin), it contains the House of Commons and the House of Lords. At the northern end of the building, partly rebuilt after damage during World War II, is St Stephen's Tower (329 feet high), containing the great bell, Big Ben. One of the major cultural, political and commercial centres of the world, London is Britain's largest city and also its capital.

▶ Beacon Hill, near Highclere Castle, Hampshire

On the summit of Beacon Hill (856 feet), overlooking Highclere Castle, are the earthwork remains of an Iron Age contour fort and the iron-railed grave of George Edward Stanhope Molyneaux Herbert, 5th Earl of Carnarvon. It was a passion for archaeology that led Carnarvon to the Valley of the Kings in Egypt, where in November 1922 he and Howard Carter discovered the tomb of Tutankhamen. A few months later the earl was bitten by a mosquito and died. Although medical experts agreed that complications and infections from the bite had caused his death, popular gossip favoured stories about 'the curse of the pharaohs'. Carnarvon was born in 1866 at Highclere Castle, designed by Charles Barry in the 1830s. Though the mansion remains the family home of the Earls of Carnarvon, it is open to the public. The Egyptian Exhibition features some of Carnarvon's Egyptian antiquities found hidden behind secret panelling (rediscovered in 1987).

▶ The Two Sisters', Reculver, Kent

Since Britain became an island in prehistoric times, wave after wave of migratory settlers from different parts of Europe have crossed the Channel through south-east England. Known as the 'Gateway to the Nation', the region is only twenty-one miles from France at its closest point, and has always, therefore, been vulnerable to invasion. In AD 43, some ninety-seven years after Gaius Julius Caesar's expeditions to Britain, the Romans invaded in force, landing at Richborough in Kent, where they quickly established a bridgehead. With a natural harbour at the southern end of the tidal Wantsum Channel (which, before being blocked by silting, separated the Isle of Thanet from the mainland), Richborough (Rutupiae) developed into a prosperous town and cross-Channel port. At Reculver, the northern end of the Wantsum Channel was guarded by the Roman fort of Regulbium. The twin towers, known as the 'Two Sisters', are twelfth-century additions to the Anglo-Saxon church of St Mary (built on the site of the fort and demolished in 1809).

▶ **Canterbury Cathedral, Kent**

During the Middle Ages the Canterbury shrine of Archbishop Thomas Becket (murdered in the cathedral on 29 December 1170) was one of Europe's most important places of pilgrimage. In 1538 Henry VIII declared Becket a traitor, and his gold-plated, jewel-encrusted tomb was plundered of its treasures and then destroyed. The monastic house (Christ Church Priory) was dissolved and the cathedral was refounded under the administration of a dean and chapter. Its foundation dates back to Anglo-Saxon times, when Canterbury was the capital of Ethelbert, King of Kent. Augustine, who had established a monastery outside the city walls in 602, founded the first cathedral inside the walls. It was this same cathedral which eventually became the primary ecclesiastical administrative centre of England. The Anglo-Saxon cathedral-priory, which had been severely damaged by the Danes in 1011 and gutted by fire in 1067, was rebuilt in 1070 by Archbishop Lanfranc with stone from Caen in France. Moreover, it has been considerably altered and rebuilt since then.

▼ **The Square and Church, Chilham, Kent**

During Caesar's second invasion of Britain in 54 BC, the Celts ambushed the advancing Romans and killed the military tribune Quintus Laberius Durus. The exact location of the attack is uncertain, but the dead Roman is said – locally – to have been buried in the Neolithic long barrow on Juliberrie Down, above the valley of the Great Stour at Chilham. Situated on the opposite side of the river some six miles south-west of Canterbury, the hill-top village stands on the site of an Iron Age camp. Whether the Romans ever built a fort on the chalk promontory is unclear, but Chilham was certainly a strategic stronghold in Anglo-Saxon times. It is traditionally held to have been the home of several Dark Age kings. The present castle comprises a Norman keep and a red-brick Jacobean mansion. The Perpendicular tower of the much-restored flint church of St Mary once supported a spire, but it was removed in 1784. The houses, shops and inns around the square date from the late fifteenth and early sixteenth centuries.

▲ Bodiam Castle, East Sussex

In the latter part of the fourteenth century French raiders gained control of the Channel and began to threaten the English coast, launching raids on many of the Cinque Ports including Rye and Winchelsea. In 1385, fearing an invasion up the estuary of the River Rother, which was navigable as far as his manor of Bodiam, Sir Edward Dalyngrigge began to build a moated castle that was both a military stronghold and a comfortable private residence. One of the last medieval castles to be built in England, Bodiam was designed in the form of a square with drum towers at each corner and a massive gateway in the centre of the north side. The castle, however, was never attacked by the French, nor is there any record of it being besieged by the English. During the Civil War the interior was demolished and, in 1916 the decaying ivy-clad shell was purchased by George Nathaniel Curzon (1st Marquis Curzon of Kedleston), who felt that 'so rare a treasure should neither be lost to our country nor desecrated by irreverent hands'. Having carried out careful restoration of the exterior, Curzon left the castle to the National Trust in 1925.

▶ South Cottage & Garden, Sissinghurst, Kent

From the forests of Hampshire and the hills of Surrey to the downlands of Sussex and the hop fields of Kent, the diversity of plant life in the south-east is so dramatic and beautiful that it can hardly be rivalled anywhere else in England. Indeed, some of the country's most celebrated landscape designers and gardeners have contributed to the region's botanical treasures. Vita Sackville-West and her husband Harold Nicolson, for instance, created the five-and-a-half-acre garden at Sissinghurst. Laid out as a series of 'outdoor rooms' around the remains of an Elizabethan mansion, the garden (now owned by the National Trust) is one of the most visited gardens in Britain. On the very day that the Nicolsons bought the property in 1930 they planted a white rose, 'Madame Alfred Carrière', against the brick wall of the South Cottage – the first building that they made habitable. The garden in front of the cottage is the most personal of all the Nicolson's 'outdoor rooms' and was considered to be their 'own little garden'.

▲ Union Mill, Cranbrook, Kent

The earliest written reference to a windmill in England is dated 1155, when Hugo de Plaiz gave the monks of Lewes the mill at his manor of Iford. Despite their apparent variety, there are three main types: the post mill (a wooden-framed structure, often with a tailpole, which rotates to face the wind around an upright centre post); the tower mill (a stationary edifice, usually brick-built, on which only the cap supporting the sweeps rotates); and the smock mill (similar to the tower mill, except that the body, or smock, is clad with weather-boarding, often painted white). One of the finest working smock mills in England towers above the rooftops of the old market town and cloth-making centre of Cranbrook, the so-called 'Capital of the Weald'. Built in 1814, it derives its name from the Union of Creditors who took over the business in 1819 when Henry Dobell, the owner, went bankrupt. Having been restored by Cranbrook Windmill Association, founded in 1982, the mill is now regularly open to the public.

▲ Bateman's, Burwash, East Sussex

One of England's earliest motoring enthusiasts, Rudyard Kipling, together with his American wife, Carrie, was driving his 'heart-breaking' Locomobile 'down an enlarged rabbit-hole of a lane' at Burwash in 1900 when they happened upon Bateman's, a 'grey stone lichened house' built in 1634 by a Sussex ironmaster. Although they both fell in love with the house on sight, feeling 'her Spirit – and Feng Shui – to be good', it was not until 1902, when the property became vacant, that they were able to secure its purchase. By 1905, with the additional purchase of adjoining farms, Kipling had increased the estate to 300 acres. In order to provide the house with electricity, he installed a turbine generator in the mill at the bottom of the garden. Together with Carrie, he was also responsible for designing much of the garden, including a shallow pond in which their children could play. Occasionally, in the visitor's book an entry is followed by the initials F.I.P., meaning 'Fell In Pond'.

▲ Fairfield Church,
Walland Marsh, Kent

Although the name 'Romney Marsh' is often applied to all the levels between Hythe and Winchelsea, Romney Marsh proper occupies the area east of a line between Appledore and New Romney, with its northernmost extremity formed by the Royal Military Canal. More accurately, therefore, the area which embraces all the marshes, including Romney, Walland, Denge and Guldeford should simply be called the Marsh. The smallest church still in use is St Thomas Becket's at Fairfield, set amidst sheep-grazed pastureland, patchworked by dykes. The date of its foundation is obscure, but a timber-framed church is known to have existed here in the thirteenth century. The building was dismantled in 1912 and painstakingly reconstructed with the addition of an outer fabric of red and blue brick. Legend says that it was built by an unnamed Archbishop of Canterbury, who accidentally fell into a dyke. Saved from drowning by a farmer, he gave thanks by erecting the church and dedicating it to his martyred predecessor.

▶ Battle Abbey, Battle, East Sussex

The last successful military invasion of England occurred in 1066, when William, Duke of Normandy, led his army ashore at Pevensey unopposed. Ten days later, at the Battle of Senlac Hill, the Anglo-Saxons under Harold II were defeated, and William the Conqueror became the first Norman king of England. As an act of atonement for the slaughter of his conquest, William erected a monastery on the hill at Battle, with the high altar of the abbey church marking the spot where Harold had been killed. The Great Gatehouse – one of the finest medieval monastic gatehouses in England – was erected in 1338, and the abbey was fortified. After its dissolution in 1538, the abbey was acquired by Sir Anthony Browne, who demolished the church, chapter house and part of the cloisters, and converted the west range, including the abbot's house, into a private mansion. Although the mansion is now occupied by Battle Abbey School, the rest of the remains, gatehouse included, are open to the public.

◀ Ashdown Forest, near Gills Lap, East Sussex

On Gills Lap – overlooking the open, Wealden heathland of Ashdown Forest, with its clumps of Scots pines, coverts of silver birch, patches of old beech and solitary oaks – is a memorial to A.A. Milne and E.H. Shepard 'who collaborated in the creation of Winnie-the-Pooh'. In 1925, five years after the birth of his son Christopher Robin, and a year after the publication of his book of children's verses entitled *When We Were Very Young*, Milne purchased Cotchford, a red-brick farmhouse near the village of Hartfield. Before Christopher left for boarding school in 1929, a further three books in the series, all illustrated by Shepard, were written: *Winnie-the-Pooh* (1926), *Now We Are Six* (1927) and *The House at Pooh Corner* (1928). Gills Lap, the highest hill in the forest at 671 feet, appears in the latter publication as 'Galleons Lap', where Christopher Robin and Pooh find an 'enchanted place'. Similarly, many other places in the stories can be identified and, inevitably, the area of forest around Gills Lap and Hartfield has now been dubbed 'Pooh Country'.

▲ Sheffield Park Garden, East Sussex

Boasting 'one of the finest collections of autumn colouring, flowering and coniferous trees and shrubs in the British Isles', Sheffield Park was originally laid out from about 1775 around a series of lakes by John Baker Holroyd (created Earl of Sheffield in 1816), under the guidance of 'Capability' Brown and later Humphry Repton. The 3rd Earl, with the assistance of his gardener William Thomas Moore, created the basic structure of the planting that exists today. On his death in 1909, the 100-acre garden was purchased by Arthur Gilstrap Soames, a wealthy brewer, who transformed it into one of the most celebrated woodland gardens in England. It was he who planted the rhododendrons for which Sheffield Park is justly famous. The neo-Gothic mansion overlooking the garden was designed by James Wyatt in 1775. Like many gardens in the south of England, Sheffield Park suffered badly from the great storm of 1987, and further damage was caused by the storm of January 1990.

▼ Lewes Castle, East Sussex

Immediately after the Conquest the Normans erected a series of strategically sited fortifications to protect and preserve their newly won territories. The castles at Arundel on the Arun, Bramber on the Adur, and Lewes on the Ouse were designed to guard vulnerable gaps in the South Downs. The first castle at Lewes was almost certainly built shortly after 1066 by William de Warenne (created 1st Earl of Surrey in c. 1087). Together with his wife Gundrada, Warenne also founded the Cluniac Priory of St Pancras at South-

over, just south of the town, which subsequently became the chief house of that Order in England. The castle, which overlooks the town and Ouse valley, originally had a single artificial motte or mound. Eventually, a second motte was constructed at the south-western end of the long, oval bailey. Although both mounds were crowned with shell keeps, only the south-western keep, erected in the early twelfth century, survives. It was strengthened with two polygonal towers in c. 1264. The barbican, or outer gateway, was built early in the fourteenth century.

▲ Parish Church, Southease, East Sussex

In 1966 the little flint church at Southease – standing above the sloping village green on the west bank of the River Ouse – celebrated one thousand years of recorded history; in 966 Edgar, King of the English, had signed a charter granting both church and manor to Hyde Abbey at Winchester. The present church dates from the early twelfth century and remained in the possession of the monastery until its dissolution in 1537. Its most obvious feature is the round tower, one of only three in Sussex (the others being St John's at Piddinghoe and St Michael's at Lewes); all are in the Ouse valley, and all date from the first half of the twelfth century. The thirteenth-century wall paintings, which once covered the entire interior walls, were revealed in 1934-5. Among the huge number of items listed in the Parish Register is an entry dated 1604, in which the rector not only records the remarriage of a widower, but, unusually, also adds his feelings on the matter, in Latin: 'A shipwrecked sailor seeks a second shipwreck.'

▲ Royal Pavilion, Brighton, East Sussex

Despite the fact that it has the oldest electric railway in Britain, England's largest man-made marina and the country's most popular pier, Brighton is world-famous because of its Royal Pavilion, created in a style more resembling an Indian mogul's palace than the elegant Regency houses of the period. Brighton's transformation from a small fishing port (known as Brighthelmstone) to one of the most fashionable resorts in the island, was begun by Dr Richard Russell, a local physician, who published a book in the 1750s extolling the beneficial effect of 'Sea Water in Diseases of the Glands', thereby encouraging people to 'take the waters'. The resort was given the royal seal of approval in 1783 with a visit by the Prince of Wales (Prince Regent in 1811 and George IV in 1820). The small farmhouse which the Prince leased was rebuilt in 1787 by Henry Holland as a classical villa with a central rotunda and dome. Further rebuilding and enlargement, culminating in the work of John Nash between 1815 and 1822, produced one of the most celebrated architectural fantasies in Europe.

◄ The Long Man of Wilmington,
East Sussex

The tall enigmatic figure of the Long Man of Wilmington is the largest human hill carving in Britain, measuring over 231 feet in height and 115 feet between staves (the one in his left hand being 241 feet long and the one in his right hand 4 feet shorter). He is also one of only two giant figures to survive on the island, the other being the Cerne Abbas Giant in Dorset. Their only similarity, however, is that they were both carved in the green turf of a chalk hill. The Long Man – sometimes called the Lanky Man or the Lone Man – stands on the steep escarpment of Windover Hill facing the village of Wilmington. In Rudyard Kipling's poem 'Sussex' (1902), he 'looks naked toward the shires'. His present appearance, which dates from 1874, and is now defined by white concrete blocks, is based on an indistinct outline 'discovered' the year before by a Dr J.S. Phene. From a rough sketch (probably unreliable, as it was made from memory) by Sir William Burrell in 1779, it seems that the earlier giant held a rake in his right hand and a scythe in his left.

▲ Church and Parsonage,
Westdean, East Sussex

Hidden amidst the trees of Friston Forest, in a fold of the South Downs between Seaford and Eastbourne, the ancient hamlet of Westdean contains an old parsonage, a flint and stone church and the ruins of a medieval manor house. The parsonage, reputed to be the oldest small medieval house still inhabited in England, was built in c. 1280 possibly by Benedictine monks from Wilmington Priory. The original building, with walls over two feet thick, was sympathetically extended in 1894. The parish church of All Saints dates from Norman times, although fragments may remain of the original Anglo-Saxon foundation. Capped by a squat gabled spire, the bell tower is partly Norman and partly fourteenth century. Tradition maintains that the manor house (demolished in the 1830s) stood on the site of Alfred the Great's palace, mentioned in the late ninth century by Asser, the king's biographer and contemporary. Within the high flint walls of the manor, opposite the church and parsonage, are the roofless remains of a circular medieval dovecote.

The line of perpendicular white cliffs stretching from Beachy Head to Cuckmere Haven, which includes the Seven Sisters, marks the meeting point of the South Downs and the English Channel. At 534 feet, Beachy Head is the highest chalk sea cliff in Britain. Known to the Normans as Beauchef or 'fair head', the headland is one of the most famous landmarks in England. Yet over the centuries many ships have foundered along this part of the coastline, and in consequence, the Belle Tout lighthouse was erected in 1831 by 'Mad Jack' Fuller of Brightling and designed by Thomas Stevenson, although it did not become operational until 1834. Standing on top of the cliffs some two miles west of Beachy Head, the light was so often obscured by low cloud and mist that it was eventually abandoned and is now a private residence. Its replacement was erected at the foot of the cliffs below Beachy Head in 1902. Painted red and white, the 142-foot-high lighthouse, which casts a powerful beam that in clear weather can be seen for twenty-five miles, switched to automatic operation in 1983.

▶ **Hatchlands Park, East Clandon, Surrey**

Three outstanding National Trust mansions – Hatchlands Park, Clandon Park and Polesden Lacey – stand on the North Downs between Guildford and Dorking. Hatchlands was built in 1757 by the architect Stiff Leadbetter, for Admiral Edward Boscawen. The interior contains the earliest recorded decoration by Robert Adam (1728–92) which, appropriately, has a nautical theme. The Palladian house of Clandon Park was built in the early 1730s by the Venetian architect Giacomo Leoni, for Thomas, 2nd Baron Onslow. The largest and most impressive room in the house is the two-storeyed marble entrance hall. The house at Polesden Lacey, owned by Richard Brinsley Sheridan (1751–1816), was replaced in the 1820s by a Regency villa, built by Joseph Bonsor to the designs of Thomas Cubitt, and much enlarged by Ambrose Poynter in 1902–6. The property, noted for the Edwardian opulence of its interiors, was once the home of the celebrated society hostess, the Hon. Mrs Ronald Greville (d. 1942), whose parties at the house were attended by the rich and famous.

▶ Village Green and Church, Brockham, Surrey

All the thousands of villages in England are different. Each one has its own individuality; its own history, character, traditions and architectural identity. At the heart of many old villages, like Brockham, near Dorking, is the cherished green, the focus of the community's life for centuries. Representing rural peace and quiet, the green is a quintessential part of the idealized English country scene: conjuring up romantic images of maypoles; cricket on lazy summer afternoons; and ducks paddling on the pond. At Brockham the green (which has the obligatory water pump, but no stocks) is the setting for what is claimed to be the biggest Guy Fawkes bonfire in Surrey. It is also said that the legendary W.G. Grace played cricket here. At the southern end of the green, near Vicarage Cottage, stands the parish church, built in 1846 by Benjamin Ferry in thirteenth-century style.

◀ West Street, Midhurst, West Sussex

On the southern banks of the River Rother, the old market town of Midhurst derives its name from its position 'amid wooded hills', the hills being the forested chalk downs to the south and the tree-covered sandstone heights to the north. After the Norman Conquest the invaders built a castle on St Ann's Hill, just east of the parish church, but only a few fragments remain. The original town, with its large rectangular marketplace, was laid out in the twelfth century to the west of the castle gates, with the church (then a chapel of neighbouring Easebourne parish) at its centre. On the corner of West Street and South Street, which meet in the Market Square, stands the Spread Eagle Hotel, a coaching inn dating from the early fifteenth century with a seven-bay front of c. 1700. Close by, the sixteenth-century Market Hall became the town's first Grammar School in 1672. On the north bank of the Rother, opposite Midhurst, are the battlemented ruins of Cowdray House, dating from the early sixteenth century.

▶ Halnaker Mill, near Boxgrove, West Sussex

The brick tower windmill standing on the summit of Halnaker Hill, five miles north-east of Chichester, was built in about 1750 by the Duke of Richmond for the use of tenant farmers and workers on the Goodwood Estate. Peter Hemming in *Windmills in Sussex* (1936) notes that safety railings were erected after a tragic accident in which a little girl was killed by one of the sweeps. The date is unspecified. In 1912, when Hilaire Belloc wrote his poem *Ha'naker Mill*, the windmill was derelict and sweepless. It was restored externally in 1934. The windmill is the oldest tower-mill in Sussex. At the foot of the hill are the remains of Halnaker House, the home of the Dukes of Richmond until the end of the eighteenth century, when the 3rd Duke moved into his new house at Goodwood, a mile or so to the west. In 1801, on the top of the downs, the Duke also laid out a racecourse, now world-famous for its 'Glorious Goodwood' meeting in July.

▲ House from Walderton, Weald & Downland Open Air Museum, Singleton, West Sussex

The rich architectural heritage of south-east England is illustrated in the Weald & Downland Open Air Museum at Singleton, where a fascinating variety of vernacular buildings has been preserved from Kent, Surrey, Sussex and Hampshire. Where possible the museum (founded in 1967) promotes the retention of threatened buildings on their original site. But if there is no alternative, providing money and space allow, properties are dismantled, moved and reconstructed in the grounds of the museum. One such property, re-erected on the site in 1979, is the flint and brick house from Walderton in West Sussex, the eastern half of which became the village post office in 1874. The original medieval timber-framed structure still survives inside the seventeenth-century exterior. The many other buildings on the museum site include Titchfield's sixteenth and early seventeenth-century Market Hall. In the woodland is a charcoal burner's hut, together with charcoal kilns at various stages of construction.

**▲ Harbour and Village,
Bosham, West Sussex**

The ancient village and medieval port of Bosham, situated on a small peninsula between two tidal creeks four miles west of Chichester, has been immortalized in the Bayeux Tapestry, which depicts events leading up to and culminating in the Norman Conquest. It was from Bosham harbour that Harold Godwineson, Earl of Wessex (soon to become Harold II, the last Saxon king of England), embarked in 1064 to visit Normandy. His departure and his ill-fated oath of allegiance to William, Duke of Normandy, are commemorated in the tapestry, as is the pre-Conquest church at Bosham (which even today retains much of the Anglo-Saxon building). According to legend, it was also at Bosham (or, alternatively, at Southampton) that King Canute failed to halt the advance of the incoming tide. In fact, the village is so low-lying that the streets flood at high tides. Although Canute's connection with Bosham is much disputed, tradition maintains that the bones of a young girl discovered in 1865 inside a stone coffin in the church are the remains of the king's daughter.

▼ Gatehouse, Titchfield Abbey, Hampshire

The ruins of Titchfield Abbey, founded by Bishop Peter des Roches for Premonstratensian canons in 1232, stand on the west bank of the River Meon, north of the small port and medieval market centre of Titchfield. In 1445 Henry VI and Margaret of Anjou were married in the abbey church. After its dissolution in 1537, Henry VIII granted the monastic buildings to Thomas Wriothesley (later 1st Earl of Southampton), who incorporated parts of the abbey into a mansion called Place House. Most of the property was demolished in 1781, but the shell of the gatehouse, together with its wings, still survives today. Described by John Leland in c. 1540 as a 'goodly gate', it was fashioned out of the nave of the abbey church. The Wriothesleys are remembered in the parish church of St Peter, where there is a magnificent Elizabethan monument to the 1st Earl and Countess and their son, the 2nd Earl. The 3rd Earl is depicted among the family's children as a small boy in armour.

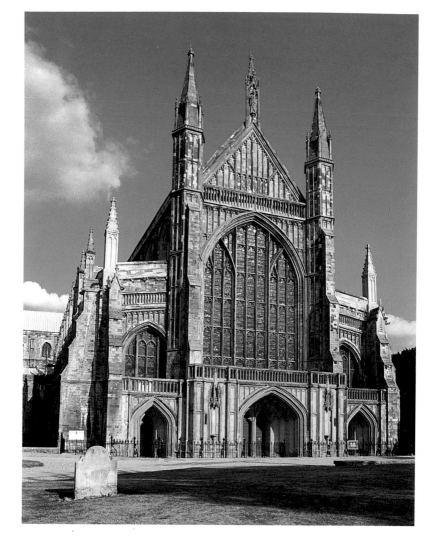

◄ Winchester Cathedral, Hampshire

The ancient city of Winchester – occupying a fold in the Hampshire downs at an important crossing-point of the River Itchen – has a hugely rich history. Standing on the site of the Roman town of Venta Belgarum, it became the capital of Wessex under Alfred the Great and, from the tenth century, it was the capital of Anglo-Saxon and Danish England: an honour it shared with London for the two hundred years that followed the Conquest. The present cathedral, which stands just south of the site of its Anglo-Saxon predecessor, founded in c. 645, was begun in 1079 by the first Norman Bishop of Winchester, Walkelin. Alterations and additions were made during the succeeding centuries, most notably by Bishops William of Edington (1345– 66) and then William of Wykeham (1367– 1404). In 1906–11 the cathedral was saved from collapse by the diver William Walker, who with his helpers underpinned the sinking foundations. Some 556 feet from east to west, it is the longest medieval cathedral in Europe.

▶ **Lyndhurst Hill, near Emery Down, New Forest, Hampshire**

In about 1079, some thirteen years after the Norman Conquest, William I created a royal hunting preserve called Nova Foresta (New Forest) in the south-west corner of Hampshire. Consisting of high windswept heathland, partly wooded scrubland and low-lying marshland, the land was exclusively reserved for the royal recreation of hunting. To protect the royal game, the king imposed very strict laws, which removed the local people's ancient rights and prevented them from interfering with the animals or their haunts. By the end of the fifteenth century, however, the emphasis had shifted from hunting to forestation. The increased demand for timber, particularly oak for ship-building, led to the enclosure of tracts of the forest as nurseries for new trees. In the latter half of the eighteenth century faster-growing softwood conifers were first introduced into what had previously been a deciduous hardwood forest of mainly oak and beech. Today the New Forest, covering an area of some 145 square miles, has been given the unofficial status of a National Park.

▶ Quay Street, Lymington, New Forest, Hampshire

Situated at the lowest crossing-point of the Lymington River, Lymington dates back to Iron Age times when the settlement was defended by two hillforts, Buckland Rings and Ampress. It is thought that the 'salterns' or salt works, which later proved to be Lymington's principal asset, were created shortly after the Norman Conquest (although the earliest record of their existence is dated 1147). When Celia Fiennes visited the sea port in the late seventeenth century the trade was at its peak, with large quantities of salt being shipped to London. Like many other smugglers, the Lymington 'free-traders' are reputed to have used subterranean passages to shift their contraband. Press-gangs operated from Harlequin Inn (now Pressgang Cottage) in Bath Road; while excise men worked out of the Old Customs House (now Hawkes

the jewellers) in Quay Street. With its Georgian houses and narrow cobbled streets, Lymington today is a busy yachting centre linked to the Isle of Wight by a cross-Solent ferry service.

▲ Furzey Gardens, Minstead, New Forest, Hampshire

Near the entrance to Furzey Gardens is a red-brick and timber-framed building, known as Forest Cottage, which is reputed to have been built in 1560 with timber from the shipyards at Lymington. Like the adjacent black weatherboarded 'Will Selwood Gallery', it is thatched with wheat reed. Furzey House, built in 1922 and now a Christian retreat, is thatched with freshwater reed, while the lakeside shelter is thatched with heather. The gardens, established in 1922 and extending to eight acres, contain a wide variety of trees and flowering shrubs, including rhododendron, azaleas, eucryphias and heathers. Furzey House and Furzey Gardens, both owned by the same charitable trust, are situated on the outskirts of the New Forest village of Minstead. The parish church of All Saints there is noted for its remarkable interior fittings – three-decker pulpit, upper and lower galleries and Georgian 'parlour pews'. The latter, built as completely separate rooms, have their own outside entrance, fireplace and chimney. Sir Arthur Conan Doyle (1859–1930) lies buried in the churchyard.

▶ Stonehenge,
Salisbury Plain, Wiltshire

The most famous prehistoric monument in Wiltshire is Stonehenge. Dating from Neolithic times, it was built in three main stages: in c. 3,000 BC there was a large circular earthwork; about 1,000 years later some eighty bluestones – weighing up to four tons each – were brought from Wales to build a temple, and arranged in two incomplete circles. The final stage saw the construction of a fully lintelled stone circle – 100 feet in diameter – using sarsen boulders weighing up to fifty tons apiece from the Marlborough Downs. The purpose of the stone circle remains a mystery.

With its rich Celtic heritage and wild, forbidding landscape of granite tors, rugged cliffs, sarcen-strewn plains and windswept moors, south-west England has long been considered a land apart. Although supporting a wealth of historical, nautical, literary and industrial sites, it is particularly noted for having the largest number of prehistoric monuments in Britain. Beneath the physical presence of many ancient sites lurks the hint of unseen forces: timeless energies stretching back into the distant past, linking one sacred centre with another. Stories and legends abound of giants, devils, mermaids and piskies, and, in more recent times, of inexplicable phenomena like corn circles. Here is the legendary realm of King Arthur; the final resting place of the Holy Grail, the magnet for missionary saints from Brittany, Ireland and Wales; the ancient 'temple' of pagan sun-worshippers or astronomers; and the source of inspiration for countless writers and artists, most notably Thomas Hardy, who wove many legends and stories into the part-real, part-imagined landscape of his Wessex novels.

The chalk downland of Salisbury Plain in Wiltshire, where Stonehenge stands proudly, covers an area of some 200 square miles, with a maximum height of 945 feet at its western edge. Bodmin Moor in Cornwall covers approximately 120 square miles, with its highest tor, Brown Willy, rising to 1,375 feet. The old coaching hostelry in the heart of the moor was immortalized by Daphne du Maurier in her novel *Jamaica Inn*. The Dartmoor National Park, designated in 1951, covers 365 square miles of Devon. Like Bodmin Moor, it consists of a moorland mass of granite, crowned by many grey, shattered tors, which have been weathered into fantastic shapes. Although its highest point is High Wilhays (2,038 feet), nearly all of the moor lies at between 1,000 and 1,500 feet. By way of contrast, the Exmoor National Park, created in 1954, is an undulating plateau of green, hedged pastures and heather-clad moorland, intersected by deep, wooded valleys. Covering 265 square miles of Devon and Somerset, with its highest point at Dunkery Beacon reaching 1,704 feet, it is the smallest of England's seven National Parks.

Beyond its physical appearance, the landscape in this once-remote region of England holds a special attraction. The unseen forces that drew people in the past continue to exert their timeless influence today.

◀ Silbury Hill, near Avebury, Wiltshire

Despite over two centuries of investigation the purpose of Silbury Hill – the largest artificial mound in Europe – remains an enigma. Dating from c. 2700 BC, it stands 130 feet high, with a base area of over five acres, and it does not appear to have been used for burial. Its construction took place in three stages, each making the mound larger and more impressive than the one before. The first mound was built on a natural terrace using layers of gravel, turf, soil, clay and chalk. This was built over in the second phase when chalk rubble was dug from around the base to create a partial ditch – forty feet wide, twenty feet deep and 350 feet in diameter. Before the second phase had been completed, however, the ditch was filled in and the

third mound – with a base diameter of 520 feet – was built, with excavated material from an even larger and deeper ditch. For the final mound the builders used chalk blocks to create a series of six huge concentric steps, one on top of the other. The smooth outline was formed by filling in the steps with a mixture of chalk rubble and silt.

▲ Great Chalfield Manor, near Melksham, Wiltshire

Considered to be one of the finest late medieval manor houses in England, Great Chalfield Manor was built of local honey-coloured stone between 1465 and 1480 by Thomas Tropnell, a wealthy Wiltshire landowner. Standing on the site of an earlier fortified build-

ing, the house, despite having a moat and fishpond, was never completely encircled by water. In 1836, when Thomas Larkin Walker, a pupil of Pugin, made a careful record of it, the property was in a ruinous state, having suffered over a century of neglect and disrepair. Some seventy years later Robert Fuller commissioned the architect Sir Harold Brakspear, to restore the house, and his sensitive reconstruction, completed in 1912, was based on Walker's drawings. The demolished south and east wings of Tropnell's manor, however, were not rebuilt. The crocketed spire on the parish church of All Saints (far left of photograph) was added by Tropnell. Robert Fuller granted the manor to the National Trust in 1943, and it is still lived in by his descendants.

▶ West Front, Wells Cathedral, Somerset

Standing on the site of an Anglo-Saxon cathedral, with an ancestry dating back to Roman times, the present building replaced a Norman cathedral consecrated in 1148. Begun in the late twelfth century, alterations and additions continued until 1508 when the south cloister was completed. The West Front, once brilliantly gilded and coloured, is adorned with hundreds of statues. It was restored after being badly damaged by Puritans in the seventeenth century, and is, in Pevsner's words, the 'richest receptacle of thirteenth century sculpture in England'. Situated at the foot of the Mendip Hills, the cathedral city and market town of Wells derives its name from the natural springs that rise in the grounds of the Bishop's Palace. The defensive moat and fortifications were added to the thirteenth-century residence by Ralph of Shrewsbury in 1331, when he was in dispute with the townspeople. Boasting many other ancient buildings of interest, Wells is England's smallest city.

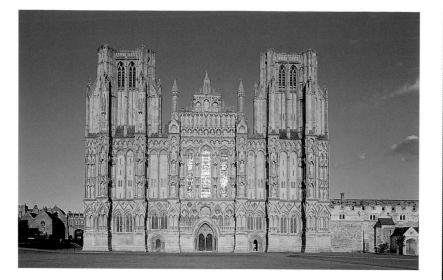

▼ Glastonbury Tor, Somerset

Glastonbury Tor – a religious centre since pre-Christian days – is considered by some modern-day pilgrims to be the holiest place in England; Joseph of Arimathea, the first-century missionary, is said to have brought the Grail here. He is said to have buried it at the foot of the tor, and it was on nearby Wearyall Hill that the staff he thrust into the ground miraculously grew into the Glastonbury Thorn, blossoming every Christmas thereafter. The tor, rising 518 feet above sea level, was once an island, surrounded by the watery wastes of the Somerset Levels. All that remains now of the medieval church of St Michael is the tower; until its dissolution in 1539, the abbey was one of the richest and most powerful religious houses in England. The alleged remains of Arthur and Guinevere were found in the graveyard in 1191, and reinterred in the church.

◄ **White Horse,**
Westbury Hill, Wiltshire

The oldest 'white horse' hill figure in Wiltshire is situated on the steep western slope of Westbury Hill, below the Iron Age hillfort of Bratton Castle. Cut into the turf in 1778, it replaced an older horse of unknown date and origin. The earlier horse was said to commemorate King Alfred's victory over the Danes at Ethandun (possibly nearby Edington) in 878; it was a strange, long-bodied, heavy-chested creature, somewhat resembling a dachshund, with short stumpy legs and a long tail curving upwards and ending in a crescent moon. Facing right, it had one round eye, two ears and wore a saddle. Evidence of the peculiar, almost comical, appearance of this giant horse, however, comes from a drawing in Gough's edition of *Camden's Britannia* (1772) and may be the product of distortion through foreshortening or embellishment, or both. The person responsible for the present left-facing horse was a certain Mr Gee (steward to the landowner Lord Abingdon) who, apparently, so disliked the original that he remodelled it on more conventional lines.

▲ Cadbury Castle,
South Cadbury, Somerset

Although several sites, including Camelford in Cornwall, have laid claim to being the Camelot of Arthurian legend, by far the best candidate is Cadbury Castle. Fragments of pottery discovered on the hill in the mid-1950s were found to match similar imported pottery dug up at Tintagel, another Arthurian site. Although the findings did not establish a positive link with the legendary king, they did prove that the hill had been occupied during the late fifth and early sixth centuries when Arthur was supposed to have existed. Excavations in 1966–70 established that the site had been occupied from Neolithic times (c. 3350 BC) for some 4,000 years. In addition to a late Bronze Age settlement and an Iron Age hillfort encompassing about eighteen acres, the hill supported a Romano-Celtic building, possibly a temple, and a fifth-century timber hall.

▶ Gold Hill, Shaftesbury, Dorset

Simply because a small boy pushed his bike up this steep, cobbled street in a Hovis television commercial, Gold Hill has become one of the most famous streets in Britain. Overlooking the Vale of Blackmoor, the thatched and tiled stone cottages are dwarfed by the massive buttressed precinct wall of the former abbey. At the top of the hill is the Town Hall, erected in 1826–7, and the parish church of St Peter's, originally built for pilgrims. Mainly Perpendicular in style the church, standing outside the abbey walls, was the oldest of eleven churches in Shaftesbury during medieval times. The monastery was founded in c. 888 by Alfred the Great for Benedictine nuns. It became a major centre for pilgrimage after the relics of the mur-

dered boy-king, Edward the Martyr, were ceremoniously brought from Wareham to the abbey church in 979. The abbey prospered to become the

richest and largest Benedictine nunnery in the land. But, after the Dissolution, the buildings were demolished and only the foundations remain.

◀ Salisbury Cathedral, Wiltshire

Salisbury Cathedral is unique among English medieval city cathedrals in several ways: it stands on a site that has never been occupied by Norman, Anglo-Saxon or earlier foundations; the main structure, having been completed in only thirty-eight years, represents a single architectural style – Early English; the precinct walls were constructed before the city streets were laid out and all building in the Close (the largest in Britain) was therefore controlled by the church authorities; and the spire, added in the fourteenth century, is the tallest in England at 404 feet. The origins of Salisbury (New Sarum) lie two miles to the north on the hill-top settlement site of Old Sarum, where there was a prehistoric fort, a Roman stronghold and an Anglo-Saxon borough with a mint. After the Conquest, the Normans constructed a cathedral and castle on the hill. The decision to abandon the hill-top in favour of a new site in the valley below was sealed when building on the new cathedral began in 1220.

▲ Kimmeridge Bay,
Isle of Purbeck, Dorset

The most important of the various raw industrial materials found in the fossil-rich cliffs at Kimmeridge Bay is the bituminous shale, known as 'blackstone' or 'Kimmeridge coal'. During the Iron Age it was worked to make bracelets and rings, and by the time the Romans came to Britain, it was being turned on lathes and carved into ornate chair and table legs. Despite giving off an oily smoke when burned, the 'coal' was also used as a fuel, notably in the early seventeenth century when there was a glassworks on the site. During the nineteenth century attempts were made to produce by-products from the shale, including varnish, pitch, paraffin wax and fertilizers. In 1858 one firm 'Wanostrocht & Co.' secured a contract to light the streets of Paris with shale-oil gas. Today the only mineral being exploited commercially at Kimmeridge is oil, drawn from two shallow wells on the west side of the bay. The boulders in the photograph are all that remains of the stone pier built by Wanostrocht & Co. in 1860, from which the shale was shipped for processing to their factory at Wareham.

▶ Stair Hole, West Lulworth, Dorset

The English landscape has undergone enormous changes throughout the immense span of time the earth has been evolving, and it is changing and evolving still. At Stair Hole in Dorset the gradual erosive action of the sea, wind and rain has bored a hole through a weak spot in the harder rocks of the Portland-Purbeck barrier to remove part of the softer beds behind. Nearby Lulworth Cove is thought to be a later stage of the same erosive process. Here the sea's advance inland has been slowed by a wall of fairly resistant chalk, yet it continues to eat into the softer Wealden Clay at the sides. Eventually, the barrier between one bay and its neighbour will disappear to create one large bay out of two separate coves. This has happened with nearby Mupe and Worbarrow Bays, and, in time, Stair Hole and Lulworth Cove will merge in the same way. The spectacular folding and buckling of the rock strata around Stair Hole, known as the 'Lulworth Crumple', was created by violent earth movements during the Tertiary mountain-building period.

▲ Village and Chapel, Abbotsbury, Dorset

Running almost in a straight line from Portland to Bridport is an eighteen-mile ridge of shingle known as Chesil Beach. Near Abbotsbury, roughly midway along its length, the raised beach is detached from the mainland and separated from it by the Fleet, a sheltered lagoon open to the sea in Portland Harbour. This eastern section, which stretches for some ten miles, lays claim to being the longest sea bar in Europe. In its entirety, the ridge is also remarkable in that the shingle progressively increases in size from west to east. The western part of the Fleet is a wildlife sanctuary encompassing the famous Swannery, established over 600 years ago by the monks of Abbotsbury abbey, which was probably founded in the 1040s. Some parts of the abbey survive today: the Great Tithe Barn (built c. 1400) and the hill-top ruins of the fifteenth-century St Catherine's Chapel. As the monastery prospered, so the village grew in size and importance. Although the monastic church of St Peter has completely disappeared, the parish church of St Nicholas (which was always for the use of the villagers, not the monks) still stands.

▲ Lighthouse, Hartland Point, Devon

Sited on a ledge below the headland of Hartland Point – some 325 feet high – at the north-western tip of Devon, there is a small white lighthouse. Opened in 1874 and converted to automatic operation in 1983, it emits a light visible for some twenty miles. With its treacherous currents, sub-merged rocks and forbidding cliffs, the Cornish and Devon coast south of Hartland Point is notoriously danger-ous to shipping. R.S. Hawker (1803–75), the eccentric poet-parson of Morwenstow, summed up the sailor's fears when he wrote:

'From Hartland Point to Padstow Light, Is a watery grave by day and by night.'

Two miles south of Hartland Point is Hartland Quay. Established in the late sixteenth century, the harbour there was eventually abandoned during the nineteenth century after the pierhead had been repeatedly demolished by the sea. An exhibition there today describes the history of the area, including some of the shipwrecks.

▶ Packhorse Bridge, Allerford, Exmoor, Somerset

Nestling beneath the richly wooded slopes of Selworthy Beacon (1,012 feet), on the eastern side of the Vale of Porlock, are the villages of Allerford, Bossington and Selworthy (part of the Holnicote Estate). Allerford is famous for its ford and adjacent packhorse bridge, dating from medieval times. The red sandstone cottage nearby, known as 'Meadowside', was originally thatched and has a number of architectural features typical of the locality, including a porch with a room above, a tall cylindrical chimney and a small external extension that is the back of a bread oven. Although most of the cottages at Bossington date from the seventeenth century, some are medieval. The doorways and windows, however, invariably date from the nineteenth century, when many of the cottages were restored. Selworthy boasts a cluster of attractive colour-washed, thatched cottages and a white-painted Perpendicular church. Set around a small green, the cottages were built in 1828 for retired estate workers.

▶ Merlin's Cave, Tintagel, Cornwall

Although there is no hard evidence to link King Arthur with Tintagel (his legendary birthplace), recent archaeological excavations at the castle site have established that during the sixth century the natural citadel was a place inhabited by kings; that it dealt in long-distance trade, notably with the eastern Mediterranean; and that the nearby cemetery was an important Christian burial site. Some 270 feet below the crumbling ruins of the twelfth-century castle is a deep cavern, said to be haunted by the ghost of Merlin. It was on the small, pebble beach outside the cavern that the wizard is reputed to have found the infant Arthur, after he had been washed ashore. Merlin also gave the future king his name and arranged for the boy to be brought up secretly by Sir Ector and his wife. After the dying Arthur had been borne away to the island of Avalon, local tradition says that his soul lived on, incarnated in the chough (now extinct in Cornwall), and that one day, like the bird, he will return.

▶ St Peter's Cathedral, Exeter, Devon

The historic city of Exeter – sited on a small hill overlooking a ford across the River Exe, or Eisca – apparently has its origins in the Iron Age, when there was a settlement. The Romans transformed the site into a walled town, the administrative capital of Isca Dumnoniorum (derived from the name of the river and that of the Celtic inhabitants). In 670 Cenwealh, the Saxon king of Wessex, founded a Benedictine monastery on the site of the Roman forum. The monastic church, refounded in 932 and destroyed by the Danes in 1003, was rebuilt again in 1019. It became a cathedral in 1050, when Bishop Leofric transferred his see from Crediton to Exeter. In 1112 Bishop William Warelwast began to build a Norman cathedral with twin towers, north and south. The present building, incorporating parts of the old (notably the towers), was begun by Bishop Branscombe in about 1275 and completed in the mid-fourteenth century. Today the cathedral is celebrated for its spectacular rib vaulting (known as 'tierceron') which stretches unbroken through both nave and choir for over 300 feet.

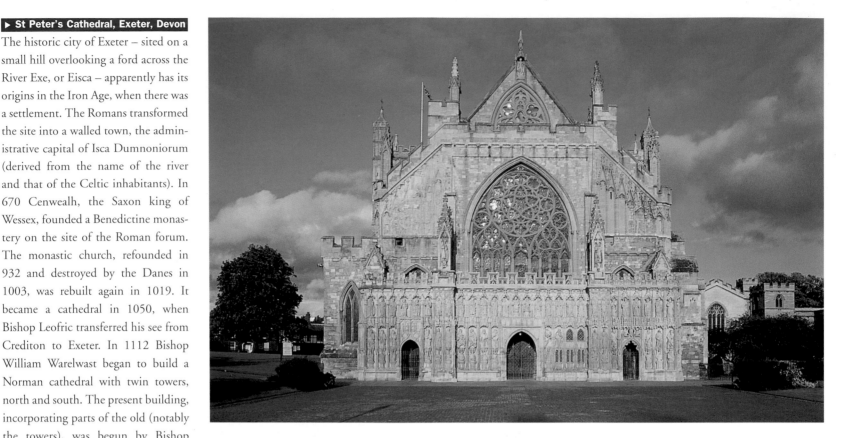

▶ Landscape, near Higher Fingle, Drewsteignton, Dartmoor, Devon

In contrast to the wild, granite upland of Dartmoor to the south, much of the landscape to the north of the River Teign is cultivated farmland, with fields enclosed by hedgebanks that are often hundreds of years old. The river itself rises in the desolate tracts of a peat bog, west of Fernworthy Forest, to flow in a semicircular curve to the English Channel at Teignmouth. Standing on a rocky spur above the wooded valley of the Teign, two miles west of the popular beauty spot of Fingle Bridge, is the imposing granite fortress of Castle Drogo. Chagford, further upstream, in addition to being one of Devon's four stannary towns, is

noted for being the home of the Dartmoor guide James Perrott who, in 1854, left a bottle (later replaced by a box) on the remote moorland of Cranmere Pool, not far from the source of the Teign. At first, visitors were simply expected to put their card in the bottle. But the idea snowballed and today hundreds of 'letterboxes' containing a rubber stamp, inkpad and visitors' book have been hidden all over Dartmoor for enthusiasts to find.

▶ A La Ronde, Exmouth, Devon

In 1796, not long after their return from a 'Grand Tour' of Europe, Jane and Mary Parminter, two spinster cousins, built the unique cottage orné, known as A La Ronde (meaning 'In the Round'). Sited on high ground overlooking the town of Exmouth and the Exe estuary, the sixteen-sided house was designed with all the rooms arranged around a central octagonal hall. Family tradition suggests that it was inspired by the Byzantine church of San Vitale at Ravenna. Emulating the basilica's celebrated mosaics, the Parminters decorated the interior walls of the gallery at the top – and the staircase leading to it – with feathers and shells of every shape, colour and size. Other rooms, particularly the drawing room, contain artwork made from sand, seaweed, shells and paper. The property (originally thatched, now tiled) was acquired by the National Trust in 1991. At the time, Gervase Jackson-Stops, the Trust's architectural adviser, described it as 'an example of Regency taste at once bizarre and intriguing, amateur and intellectual, rustic and cosmopolitan'.

▶ Bowerman's Nose, Manaton, Dartmoor, Devon

About a mile north of Hound Tor – one of almost 200 tors that crown the high moorland mass of Dartmoor – is a prominent stack of fissured granite thirty feet high, known as Bowerman's Nose. Over thousands of years the rock has cracked and weathered into a formation with an almost human profile. Although 'Bowerman' is thought to be derived from the Celtic vawr-maen meaning 'great stone', local legend maintains that he was a Norman archer, who lived near Manaton. A great hunter, he and his pack of hounds were turned to stone, either for persisting to hunt on the Sabbath or for disturbing a coven of witches. The petrified shapes of his pack of hounds

in full cry is, of course, Hound Tor. The huge, fractured granite outcrop is reputedly also the haunt of one of a number of phantom black hounds from Hell, which raced across the moor to howl around the Buckfastleigh tomb of Richard Cabell. The story of Squire Cabell, who died in 1677 having sold his soul to the Devil, is said to have provided the inspiration and setting for Arthur Conan Doyle's *The Hound of the Baskerville's*.

▶ **Stone Rows, Merrivale, Dartmoor, Devon**

The bleak, windswept plateau of the Dartmoor National Park contains the greatest concentration of Bronze Age monuments in Europe. Scattered throughout the landscape are the remains of countless prehistoric villages, huts, walled enclosures, menhirs (standing stones), kistvaens (burial chambers), stone circles and stone rows. Although it is thought that the menhirs, circles and rows had some religious or ceremonial function, their true purpose remains unproven. Perhaps the most enigmatic are the stone rows, of which there are around seventy. Most of these granite 'avenues' or 'alignments' consist of either single or double rows, but there are a few triples. The longest, located seven miles south-east of Merrivale, runs north for some two miles from a stone circle on Stall Moor, across the River Erme to Green Hill. Of the three at Merrivale, two run more or less parallel with each other in an east-west direction (one for 596 feet, the other for 865 feet). Nearby are several burial cairns, a menhir and a stone circle.

▲ **Church and Village, Widecombe-in-the-Moor, Dartmoor, Devon**

Immortalized in the song 'Widdicombe Fair' (first published in 1880), Widecombe-in-the-Moor lies in the valley of the East Webburn River, six miles west of Bovey Tracey. During the fifteenth and sixteenth centuries the village was a prosperous tin-mining centre, and it was during this period that the high tower (120 feet) was added to the fourteenth-century parish church. Hanging on wooden boards inside the church is a poem, written by the village schoolmaster, which describes a terrifying event which took place during a service on Sunday 21 October 1638. After the tower had been struck by lightning, causing part of it to fall through the roof, a huge fireball shot through the church, killing four of the worshippers and injuring a great many more. Hill considered the tragedy to be an act of God, but others maintained that the Devil caused the explosion, crashing through the roof to seize someone in the congregation who had fallen asleep.

▲ Wistman's Wood, Two Bridges, Dartmoor, Devon

Reputed to be one of the most haunted places in Dartmoor, Wistman's Wood – with its strangely gnarled and stunted oaks – lies 1,300 feet above sea level in the valley of the West Dart River. The trees, primarily pedunculate oak, are on average about fifteen feet high, and grow from crevices in a jumble of granite boulders, known as clitter, strewn across the hillside. The most ancient oaks are about five hundred years old, and, like everything in the wood, the twisted trunks and branches are covered with a rich velvet blanket of mosses, lichens, liverworts and ferns. Similar ancient woods can be found at Black Tor Copse and Piles Copse. Once thought to have been a sacred grove of the Druids, Wistman's Wood is associated with the Devil's Wisht Hounds, spectral black dogs with red eyes. They emerge from the trees at midnight, supposedly led by Satan riding a headless black horse, and anyone seeing them is doomed to die within a year. The eight-acre wood, owned by the Duchy of Cornwall, is now a nature reserve.

▶ Tavistock, from Whitchurch Common, Devon

Having grown up around the Benedictine Abbey that had been founded in the tenth century, the ancient town of Tavistock was granted its first market charter in the early twelfth century by Henry I. In 1281, because of a boom in Dartmoor tin, it became a stannary or coinage town – one of four in Devon where the miners had to bring their tin to be weighed, or 'coigned', stamped and assayed for duty. It also became an important centre for the wool and cloth trade, and, from c. 1790–1870, it prospered on copper mining. After the Dissolution of the Monasteries in 1539, the abbey and town became the property of the Russells, later Dukes of Bedford. During the nineteenth century, with wealth from his mining interests, the 7th Duke, rebuilt the town centre, using the local grey-green Hurdwick stone. Tavistock's port on the River Tamar – to which, from 1817, it was linked by a four-mile canal was Morwellham Quay, now an open-air industrial museum complex, re-creating 'the Greatest Copper Port in Queen Victoria's Empire'.

▲ Buckfast Abbey, Buckfastleigh, Dartmoor, Devon

First founded as a Benedictine monastery in 1018 by King Canute, Buckfast Abbey was refounded for Savigniac monks in 1136. It became a Cistercian house eleven years later, when the Savigniac and Cistercian Orders were united. After the Dissolution of the Monasteries in 1539 most of the buildings were destroyed. The property was purchased by an exiled community of French Benedictine monks in 1882, and twenty-four years later the abbot, Dom Anscar Vonier, decided to rebuild the abbey. The church was consecrated in 1932 and the tower completed in 1938. Shortly afterwards Abbot Vonier died, his work completed. Today the abbey houses a working community of monks, many of whom have become experts in their chosen field. Brother Adam, for instance, joined the community in 1910, at the age of twelve, and became a world authority on bee-keeping and honey production. He also bred a new strain of bee known as the 'Buckfast bee', which has the qualities of being disease resistant, reluctant to swarm or sting, and is a prolific producer of honey.

▲ Polperro, from Downend Point, Cornwall

One of the most popular fishing villages in Cornwall, Polperro lies at the foot of a steep wooded coombe, its narrow streets and alleyways running down to a small harbour. Once known as 'Polstink' because of the smell of pilchards, the village was a notorious haunt of smugglers. According to Jonathan Couch, grandfather of Arthur Quiller-Couch or 'Q', Polperro was 'probably a stronghold of the contraband trade in early times'. Indeed, the boats, specially built to outrun the customs authorities, were well able to 'offer them a tow-rope in derision'. In an attempt to stop the activities of the 'fair-traders', one of the first resident excise units was established in the village. Unable to find anyone willing to give them lodgings, the officials were forced to live in 'the hull of a vessel moored to the old quay'. Exhibits of Polperro's smuggling past are on display today in a small museum. Jonathan Couch was born in the village in 1789 and lived in Couch's House for many years. Sam Puckey decorated the outside of the Shell House in the Warren with shells between 1937 and 1942.

▶ Fowey Estuary, from Bodinnick, Cornwall

In his Survey of Cornwall (1602), Carew describes the estuary as a: 'fair and commodious haven, where the tide daily presenteth his double service of flowing and ebbing, to carry and recarry whatsoever the inhabitants shall be pleased to charge him withal, and his creeks (like a young wanton lover) fold about the land, with many embracing arms.'

He also mentions that the entrance to the harbour was guarded by block-houses. St Catherine's Castle (on the right of the photograph), dating from 1539 to 1542, was one of a chain of fortresses built on the orders of Henry VIII, to protect the south coast from a feared French invasion. The block-house, on the opposite headland was built after a French raid in 1457. The historic town of Fowey, once a centre for piracy, takes its name from the river which rises on Bodmin Moor, flows through the medieval port of Lostwithiel, and enters the sea beyond St Catherine's Point.

▶ Baptistry, Menacuddle, near St Austell, Cornwall

Innumerable towns, villages, parishes, churches and holy wells have been dedicated to the missionaries who brought Celtic (rather than Roman) Christianity to Cornwall during the fifth and sixth centuries. Little wonder, it is said, that there are more saints in the county than there are in heaven. Some, like St Mewan and his disciple St Austell, migrated from Wales to Brittany by way of Cornwall. The two adjoining parishes of St Mewan and St Austell are named after them. The saints were apparently such close companions that, allegedly, they died within a week of each other and were buried in the same tomb in the monastery of Saint-Mèen (founded by Mewan) in Brittany. For his baptisms and ministrations in mid-Cornwall Austell is reputed to have used the holy well at Menacuddle (meaning 'rock well'). The site, located less than a mile north of the old market town and china-clay centre of St Austell, is now occupied by a small granite baptistry which dates back to the fifteenth century.

▼ Walsingham Place and the Cathedral, Truro, Cornwall

During the Middle Ages the city of Truro was an important stannary town, a prosperous market centre and an inland port, flourishing particularly on the export of tin. The town's ancient right of jurisdiction over the whole of the Truro and Fal estuary, however, was successfully challenged by Falmouth in 1709, and thereafter, together with the silting up of the Truro River, it declined as a port. During the eighteenth and nineteenth

centuries, Truro became a fashionable centre for the wealthy, and many fine mansions and houses were built during this period, including Walsingham Place, a small Georgian crescent. In 1877 Queen Victoria granted Truro city status, and three years later work began on building the cathedral. Designed by John Loughborough Pearson in the Early English Gothic style, it was completed in 1910. The south aisle of the sixteenth-century parish church of St Mary was incorporated into the structure, and a chapter house was added in 1967.

▲ St Michael's Chapel, Roche Rock, Cornwall

Sometimes, when storms sweep in from the Atlantic and violent waves smash against the granite cliffs, the troubled spirit of Cornwall's most famous ghost – John, or Jan, Tregeagle – can be heard howling in the wind. Possibly an historical figure, Tregeagle is said to have been a dishonest lawyer, who not only embezzled his clients' money and murdered his wife and children, but sold his soul to the Devil. Although he was buried in consecrated ground (the result of a bribe), his spirit was condemned to eternal punishment. One tale has him flapping like a giant bird around the cliffs of Land's End, luring the unwary to their death. At Roche Rock, on the northern edge of Hensbarrow Downs, overlooking the white pyramids of china clay country, he is found tormenting one of the holy men who occupied the hermitage. Trying to seek sanctuary from the demons chasing him, he thrust his head through the chapel window. Nevertheless only magic spells could silence his screams.

▲ Loe Bar, Porthleven, Cornwall

Located within the 'claw' of Cornwall, midway between Porthleven and Gunwalloe, Loe Pool – the county's largest freshwater lake – is separated from the sea by the shingle barrier of Loe Bar. Originally, the Loe was the estuary of the River Cober which flows through the once-thriving port of Helston, some two miles inland. By the thirteenth century the bar had completely formed and Helston was cut off from the sea. Almost all the shingle is composed of flint and, as there are no land deposits of the stone along the southern Cornish coast, one can only presume that it originates from somewhere offshore. According to one story, the bar was formed by the contents of a sack dropped by John Tregeagle. The spillage (whether deliberate or accidental is unrecorded) occurred during an act of penance which required the tormented spirit to move sand from Gunwalloe to Porthleven. Loe Pool is also associated with Arthurian legend and is one of two lakes in Cornwall into which Sir Bedivere might have cast Excalibur.

▲ Men-an-Tol, near Morvah, Cornwall

The wild, grey granite peninsular of Land's End contains one of the greatest concentrations of prehistoric monuments in Britain. More than 1,200 sites have been recorded within an area of 87 square miles, and 800 of these can still be seen. Among the ancient monuments on the high moors east of Morvah, is a round-holed stone, known as the Men-an-Tol, meaning 'stone of the hole'. Flanked by two upright stones, it has a diameter of about four feet and is thought to date from the Bronze Age. Its purpose is a complete mystery, but the most popular theory suggests that it was the port-hole entrance to a tomb, now lost. Close by is a fourth stone, now fallen. None of the stones may now be in their original position. Also known as the 'Crick Stone', the Men-an-Tol was believed to possess magical and curative powers.

▲ Armed Knight and the Longships Lighthouse, Land's End, Cornwall

Land's End has two contrasting reputations: on the one hand it is a tourist Mecca, the westernmost point in mainland England and Wales, and the end of the 900-mile (approx.) walk from John O'Groats; on the other, it is an offshore graveyard for countless wrecks, with treacherous currents, hidden reefs and jagged rocks making passage extremely hazardous to shipping. About a mile and a half offshore, the Longships Lighthouse has a white light on the seaward side, and a red light on the landward. The first lighthouse to be sited here (the subject of a painting by J.M.W. Turner in 1834) was built in 1795; it was replaced in 1873. Twenty-eight miles offshore lie the Isles of Scilly. According to legend these islands are the western peaks of the lost land of Lyonesse (thought to be identical with Liones, the home of Tristan, one of the Knights of the Round Table). Its cities and churches – like those of Atlantis – lie submerged beneath the sea. In addition to the tourist attractions at Land's End, there is a hotel and the 'First and Last House'.

ENGLISH HERITAGE

All English Heritage properties, except where specified, are open every day throughout the year, excluding 24–26 December and 1 January.

HEAD OFFICE
Keysign House, 429 Oxford Street
London W1R 2HD
Tel: (0171) 973 3000

HISTORIC PROPERTIES NORTH
Bessie Surtees House, 41–44 Sandhill
Newcastle Upon Tyne NE1 3JF
Tel: (0191) 261 1585

HISTORIC PROPERTIES MIDLANDS
Hazelrigg House, 33 Marefair
Northampton NN1 1SR
Tel: (01604) 730320

HISTORIC PROPERTIES LONDON
Kenwood, Hampstead Lane
London NW3 7JR
Tel: (0181) 348 1286

HISTORIC PROPERTIES SOUTH WEST
7–8 King Street
Bristol
Avon BS1 4EQ
Tel: (0117) 9750700

HISTORIC PROPERTIES SOUTH EAST
1 High Street
Tonbridge
Kent TN9 1SG
Tel: (01732) 778000

AVEBURY MUSEUM
Avebury
Wiltshire SNH 1RF
Tel: (01672) 539250

BARNARD CASTLE
Barnard
County Durham DL12 0AT
Tel: (01833) 638212
Open April to end October daily; November to March, Wednesdays to Sundays.

BATTLE ABBEY
High Street
Battle
East Sussex TN33 0AD
Tel: (01424) 773792

CASTLE ACRE PRIORY
Castle Acre, Stocks Green
Kings Lynn
Norfolk PE32 2AF
Tel: (01760) 755394
Open April to end October daily; November to March, Wednesdays to Saturdays.

DUNSTANBURGH CASTLE
Craster
Northumberland
Tel: (01665) 576231
Open April to October daily; November to March, Wednesdays to Sundays.

GOODRICH CASTLE
Goodrich, Ross-on-Wye
Hereford & Worcester HR9 6HY
Tel: (01600) 890538

KENILWORTH CASTLE
Kenilworth
Warwickshire CV8 1NE
Tel: (01926) 52078

ORFORD CASTLE
Orford
near Woodbridge
Suffolk IP12 2ND
Tel: (013944) 50472

STONEHENGE
Amesbury
Wiltshire SP4 7DE
Tel: (01980) 623108 or 624715

TINTAGEL CASTLE
Tintagel
Cornwall PL34 0AA
Tel: (01840) 770328

WHITBY ABBEY
Whitby
North Yorkshire YO22 4JT
Tel: (01947) 603568

NATIONAL TRUST

HEAD OFFICE
36 Queen Anne's Gate
London SW1H 9AS
Tel: (0171) 222 9251

CORNWALL REGIONAL OFFICE
Lanhydrock
Bodmin
Cornwall PL30 4DE
Tel: (01208) 74281/4

DEVON REGIONAL OFFICE
Killerton House
Broadclyst
Exeter EX5 3LE
Tel: (01392) 881691

EAST ANGLIA REGIONAL OFFICE
Blickling
Norwich NR11 6NF
Tel: (01263) 733471

EAST MIDLANDS REGIONAL OFFICE
Clumber Park Stableyard
Worksop
Nottinghamshire S80 3BE
Tel: (01909) 486411

KENT & EAST SUSSEX REGIONAL OFFICE
The Estate Office
Scotney Castle
Lamberhurst
Tunbridge Wells
Kent TN3 8JN
Tel: (01892) 890651

MERCIA REGIONAL OFFICE
Attingham Park
Shrewsbury
Shropshire SY4 4TP
Tel: (01743) 709343

NORTHUMBRIA REGIONAL OFFICE
Scots' Gap
Morpeth
Northumberland NE61 4EG
Tel: (01670) 774691

NORTH-WEST REGIONAL OFFICE
The Hollens
Grasmere
Ambleside
Cumbria LA22 9QZ
Tel: (015394) 35599

SEVERN REGIONAL OFFICE
Mythe End House
Tewkesbury
Gloucestershire. GL20 6EB
Tel: (01684) 850051

SOUTHERN REGIONAL OFFICE
Polesden Lacey
Dorking
Surrey RH5 6BD
Tel: (01372) 453401

THAMES & CHILTERNS REGIONAL OFFICE
Hughenden Manor
High Wycombe
Buckinghamshire HP14 4LA
Tel: (01494) 528051
Wessex Regional Office

EASTLEIGH COURT
Bishopstrow
Warminster
Wiltshire BA12 9HW
Tel: (01985) 843600

YORKSHIRE REGIONAL OFFICE
Goddards, 27 Tadcaster Road
Dringhouses
York YO2 2QG
Tel: (01904) 702021

A LA RONDE
Summer Lane
Exmouth
Devon EX8 5BD
Tel: (01395) 265514
Open April to end October, Sundays to Thursdays.

BATEMAN'S
Burwash
Etchingham
East Sussex
TN19 7DS
Tel: (01435) 882302
Open April to end October, Saturdays to Wednesdays and Good Fridays.

BODIAM CASTLE
Bodiam
near Robertsbridge
East Sussex TN32 5UA
Tel: (01580) 830436
Open mid February to end October daily; November to early January (including New Year's Day), Tuesdays to Sundays; closed 24–26 December.

CHARLECOTE PARK
Wellesbourne
Warwickshire CV35 9ER
Tel: (01789) 470277
Open April to end October, Fridays to Tuesdays.

CLANDON PARK
West Clandon
Guildford
Surrey GU4 7RQ
Tel: (01483) 222482
Open April to end October, Saturdays to Wednesdays and Good Fridays

GREAT CHALFIELD MANOR
near Melksham
Wiltshire SN12 8NJ
Tel: (01985) 843600
Open April to end October, Tuesdays to Thursdays.

HATCHLANDS PARK
East Clandon
Guildford
Surrey GU4 7RT
Tel: (01483) 222482
Open early April to end October, Tuesdays to Thursdays, Sundays and Bank Holiday Mondays (and Fridays in August).

HIDCOTE MANOR GARDEN
Hidcote Bartrim
near Chipping Campden
Gloucestershire GL55 6LR
Tel: (01386) 438333
Open April to end October, daily except Tuesdays and Fridays.

HILL TOP
Near Sawrey
Ambleside
Cumbria LA22 0LF
Tel: (015394) 36269
Open April to end October, Saturdays to Wednesdays and Good Fridays.

HOUGHTON MILL
Houghton
near Huntingdon
Cambridgeshire PE17 2AZ
Tel: (01480) 301494
Open April to mid October, Saturdays,
Sundays and Bank Holiday Mondays; and
late June to early September, Mondays to
Wednesdays.

LINDISFARNE CASTLE
Holy Island
Berwick-upon-Tweed
Northumberland TD15 2SH
Tel: (01289) 89244
Open April to end October, Saturdays to
Thursdays and Good Fridays.

LOWER BROCKHAMPTON
Bringsty
Hereford & Worcester WR6 5UH
Tel: (01885) 488099
Open Easter to end October, Wednesdays
to Sundays, and Bank Holiday Mondays.

POLESDEN LACEY
near Dorking
Surrey RH5 6BD
Tel: (01372) 458203 or 452048
House open April to end October,
Wednesdays to Sundays and Bank Holiday
Mondays; March, weekends only;
grounds, open daily all year.

SHEFFIELD PARK GARDEN
Sheffield Park
near Uckfield
East Sussex TN22 3QX
Tel: (01825) 790231
Open April to early November, Tuesdays
to Sundays and Bank Holiday Mondays;
early November to mid December,
Wednesdays to Saturdays; March, week-
ends only.

SISSINGHURST GARDEN
Sissinghurst
near Cranbrook
Kent TN17 2AB
Tel: (01580) 712850
Open April to mid October, Tuesdays to
Sundays.

SNOWSHILL MANOR
near Broadway
Hereford & Worcester WR12 7JU
Tel: (01386) 852410
Open April to October, Wednesdays to
Mondays; closed Good Fridays.

WICKEN FEN
Lode Lane
Wicken
Ely
Cambridgeshire CB7 5XP
Tel: (01353) 720274
Open Fen daily throughout the year,
except 25 December; Cottage, April to
October, Sundays and Bank Holiday
Mondays.

NATIONAL PARKS

THE BROADS
The Broads Authority
Thomas Harvey House, 18 Colegate
Norwich
Norfolk NR3 1BQ
Tel: (01603) 610734

DARTMOOR NATIONAL PARK
AUTHORITY
Parke, Haytor Road
Bovey Tracey
Devon TQ13 9JQ
Tel: (01626) 832093

EXMOOR NATIONAL PARK
AUTHORITY
Exmoor House
Dulverton
Somerset TA22 9HL
Tel: (01398) 323665

PEAK NATIONAL PARK
Aldern House, Baslow Road
Bakewell
Derbyshire DE45 1AE
Tel: (01629) 816200

LAKE DISTRICT NATIONAL PARK
Brockhole
Windermere
Cumbria LA23 1LJ
Tel: (015394) 46601

NORTH YORK MOORS NATIONAL
PARK
The Old Vicarage
Bondgate
Helmsley
York YO6 5BP
Tel: (01439) 770657

YORKSHIRE DALES NATIONAL
PARK
Colvend
Hebden Road
Grassington
Skipton
North Yorkshire BD23 5LB
Tel: (01756) 752748

NORTHUMBERLAND NATIONAL
PARK
Eastburn
South Park
Hexham
Northumberland NE36 1BS
Tel: (01434) 605555

SHAKESPEARE BIRTHPLACE
TRUST
All properties are open daily throughout
the year except 24–26 December.

ANNE HATHAWAY'S COTTAGE
Cottage Lane
Shottery
Stratford-upon-Avon
Warwickshire CV37 9HH
Tel: (01789) 292100

SHAKESPEARE'S BIRTHPLACE
Henley Street
Stratford-upon-Avon
Warwickshire CV37 6QW
Tel: (01789) 204016

HALL'S CROFT
Old Town
Stratford-upon-Avon
Warwickshire CV37 6BG
Tel: (01789) 292107

MARY ARDEN'S HOUSE AND
COUNTRYSIDE MUSEUM
Wilmcote
Stratford-upon-Avon
Warwickshire CV37 9UN
Tel: (01789) 293455

NEW PLACE AND NASH'S HOUSE
Chapel Street
Stratford-upon-Avon
Warwickshire CV37 6EP
Tel: (01789) 292325

MISCELLANEOUS

BAMBURGH CASTLE
Bamburgh
Northumberland NE69 7DF
Tel: (01668) 214208
Open April to end October daily

BUCKFAST ABBEY
Buckfastleigh
Devon TQ11 0EE
Tel: (01364) 643301
Open daily throughout the year.

CASTLE HOWARD
York YO6 7DA
Tel: (01653) 648444
Open April to end October daily

CHATSWORTH
Bakewell
Derbyshire DE45 1PP
Tel: (01246) 582204
Open April to end October daily.

DOVE COTTAGE
The Wordsworth Trust
Grasmere
Cumbria LA22 9SH
Tel: (015394) 35544 or 35547
Open February to December, except
24–26 December.

FURZEY GARDENS
Minstead
near Lyndhurst
Hampshire
Tel: (01703) 812464
Open daily except 25 and 26 December.

IRONBRIDGE GORGE MUSEUM
(Visitor Information Service)
Ironbridge
Telford
Shropshire TF8 7AW
Tel: (01952) 433522 or (01952)
432751/432166 (weekends)
Open daily throughout the year except 24
and 25 December; some small sites closed
from November to March.

LEVENS HALL
Kendal
Cumbria LA8 0PD
Tel: (015395) 60321
Open April to end September except
Fridays and Saturdays.

LEWES CASTLE
Barbican House
Lewes
East Sussex BN7 1YE
Tel: (01273) 486290
Open all year; closed 25–26 December.

ROYAL PAVILION
Old Steine
Brighton
East Sussex BN1 1EE
Tel: (01273) 603005
Open all year; closed 25–26 December.

SHELDONIAN THEATRE
Broad Street
Oxford OX1 3AZ
Tel: (01865) 277299

WARWICK CASTLE
Warwick
Warwickshire CV34 4QU
Tel: (01926) 495421
Open every day except Christmas Day.

WATERFALL AND HERMITAGE
St Nectan's Glen
Tintagel
Cornwall PL34 0BE
Tel: (01840) 770760
Open daily throughout the year.

WEALD AND DOWNLAND
OPEN AIR MUSEUM
Singleton
Chichester
West Sussex PO18 0EU
Tel: (01243) 811348
Open all year but only Wednesdays,
Saturdays and Sundays between November
and February.

PHOTOGRAPHIC INFORMATION

The Photographic information refers to: Make and type of camera; Film size; Film stock; Tripod or Handheld; Lens; f-stop; shutter speed; Polarising filter (if used). All lenses had a filter attached primarily to protect the front element, but chosen to have a slight warming quality. The tripod was a Linhof with a large Manfrotto pan-and-tilt head, and the light meter a hand-held Seconic.

All equipment was carried in a standard rucksack.

THE NORTH–EAST

20–1 Pentax 6x7; Fuji50D; Tripod; 45mm; f22; 1/2sec

22–3 Hasselblad 503CX; 6x6; Velvia; Tripod; 80mm; f22; 1/8sec

23 Hasselblad 503CX; 6x6; Velvia; Tripod; 80mm; f22; 4sec

24 Hasselblad 503CX; 6x6; Velvia; Tripod; 80mm; f11; 1/30sec

25 Hasselblad 503CX; 6x6; Velvia; Tripod; 80mm; f22; 1/4sec; Polariser

26 (top) Hasselblad 503CX; 6x6; Velvia; Tripod; 80mm; f22; 1/4sec; Polariser

26 (bottom) Fuji GX680; 6x8; Velvia; Tripod; 210mm; f22; 1/4sec

27 Fuji GX680; 6x8; Velvia; Tripod; 210mm; f22; 1/4sec

28 (top) Nikon F3; 35mm; Fuji50D; Handheld; 180mm; f4; 1/25sec

28 (bottom) Fuji GX680; 6x8; Velvia; Tripod; 300mm; f16; 1/8sec

29 Fuji GX680; 6x8; Velvia; Tripod; 210mm; f16; 1/8sec

30 Fuji GX680; 6x8; Velvia; Tripod; 210mm; f32; 4sec

31 Fuji GX680; 6x8; Velvia; Tripod; 300mm; f16; 1/4sec

32 (top) Fuji GX680; 6x8; Velvia; Tripod; 210mm; f22; 1/4sec

32 (bottom) Fuji GX680; 6x8; Velvia; Tripod; 65mm; f22; 1/2sec; Polariser

33 Fuji GX680; 6x8; Velvia; Tripod; 65mm; f32; 1/2sec

34–5 Pentax 6x7; Fuji50D; Tripod; 45mm; f22; 1/2sec; Polariser

35 Pentax 6x7; Fuji50D; Tripod; 45mm; f22; 1/2sec; Polariser

36–7 Fuji GX680; 6x8; Velvia; Tripod; 65mm; f22; 1sec

37 (top) Nikon F3; 35mm; Velvia; Tripod; 180mm; f11; 1/30sec

37 (bottom) Pentax 6x7; Fuji50D; Tripod; 45mm; f22; 1/4sec

38–9 Pentax 6x7; Fuji50D; Tripod; 75mm; f16; 1/4sec

38 Pentax 6x7; Fuji50D; Tripod; 200mm; f22; 1sec

39 Pentax 6x7; Fuji50D; Tripod; 45mm; f22; 1/4sec

40 Fuji GX680; 6x8; Velvia; Tripod; 300mm; f11; 1/15sec

41 (top) Nikon F3; 35mm; Fuji50D; Tripod; 300mm; f5.6; 1/25sec

41 (bottom) Fuji GX680; 6x8; Velvia; Tripod; 210mm; f32; 1/4sec

42 (top) Nikon F3; 35mm; Fuji50D; Handheld; 24mm; f5.6; 1/30sec; Polariser

42 (bottom) Pentax 6x7; Fuji50D; Tripod; 45mm; f22; 1/2sec; Polariser

43 (top) Nikon F3; 35mm; Velvia; Handheld; 24mm; f5.6; 1/60sec; Polariser

43 (bottom) Fuji GX680; 6x8; Velvia; Tripod; 65mm; f22; 1/4sec

THE NORTH–WEST

44–5 Loughrigg Tarn, near Skelwith Bridge, Cumbria
Pentax 6x7; Fuji50D; Tripod; 75mm; f22; 1/8sec

46 Over Water, near Uldale, Cumbria
Pentax 6x7; Fuji50D; Tripod; 75mm; f22; 1/4sec

46–7 Loweswater, Cumbria
Pentax 6x7; Fuji50D; Tripod; 75mm; f22; 1/4sec

48–9 Buttermere and Crummock Water, from Fleetwith Pike, Cumbria
Pentax 6x7; Fuji50D; Tripod; 75mm; f8; 1/60sec

49 Derwentwater and Jaws of Borrowdale, Cumbria
Fuji GX680; 6x8; Velvia; Tripod; 80mm; f22; 4sec

50 (top) Hindscarth and Robinson, Newlands Valley, Cumbria
Pentax 6x7; Fuji50D; Tripod; 75mm; f22; 1/2sec; Polariser

50 (bottom) Whelpside Gill, Thirlmere, Cumbria
Pentax 6x7; Fuji50D; Tripod; 45mm; f22; 2sec

51 Honister Quarry, Honister Crag, Cumbria
Pentax 6x7; Fuji50D; Tripod; 45mm; f22; 1/2sec; Polariser

52–3 Pentax 6x7; Fuji50D; Tripod; 75mm; f22; 1/4sec

53 Pentax 6x7; Fuji50D; Tripod; 75mm; f22; 1sec; Polariser

54–5 Pentax 6x7; Fuji50D; Tripod; 200mm; f16; 4sec

54 Pentax 6x7; Fuji50D; Tripod; 75mm; f22; 1sec

56 (top) Pentax 6x7; Fuji50D; Tripod; 45mm; f22; 1/15sec

56 (bottom) Pentax 6x7; Fuji50D; Tripod; 75mm; f16; 1/15sec

57 Pentax 6x7; Fuji50D; Tripod; 200mm; f16; 1/4sec

58–9 Pentax 6x7; Fuji50D; Tripod; 45mm; f16; 1/4sec

60 Pentax 6x7; Fuji50D; Tripod; 200mm; f16; 1/4sec

61 Pentax 6x7; Fuji50D; Tripod; 75mm; f22; 1/2sec

62–3 Pentax 6x7; Fuji50D; Tripod; 200mm; f16; 1/8sec

63 Fuji GX680; 6x8; Velvia; Tripod; 210mm; f16; 1/8sec

64 Pentax 6x7; Fuji50D; Tripod; 75mm; f22; 1/2sec

65 (top) Pentax 6x7; Fuji50D; Tripod; 75mm; f22; 1sec

65 (bottom) Pentax 6x7; Fuji50D; Tripod; 75mm; f22; 1/4sec

66 (top) Fuji GX680; 6x8; Velvia; Tripod; 210mm; f22; 1/2sec

66 (bottom) Pentax 6x7; Fuji50D; Tripod; 75mm; f22; 1/15sec

67 (top) Pentax 6x7; Fuji50D; Tripod; 75mm; f22; 1/4sec; Polariser

67 (bottom) Pentax 6x7; Fuji50D; Tripod; 75mm; f22; 1/15sec

THE MIDLANDS

68–9 Pentax 6x7; Fuji50D; Tripod; 45mm; f22; 1/8sec

70–1 Hasselblad 503CX; 6x6; Velvia; Tripod; 150mm; f4; 1/250sec

71 Hasselblad 503CX; 6x6; Velvia; Tripod; 80mm; f8; 1/60sec

72 Hasselblad 503CX; 6x6; Velvia; Tripod; 80mm; f11; 1/15sec

72–3 Hasselblad 503CX; 6x6; Velvia; Tripod; 50mm; f16; 1/8sec

74 (top) Hasselblad 503CX; 6x6; Velvia; Tripod; 80mm; f16; 1/4sec

74 (bottom) Hasselblad 503CX; 6x6; Velvia; Tripod; 50mm; f22; 1/4sec

75 Hasselblad 503CX; 6x6; Velvia; Tripod; 50mm; f8; 1/60sec

76 (top) Nikon F3; 35mm; Velvia; Handheld; 85mm; f5.6; 1/60sec

76 (bottom) Nikon F3; 35mm; Velvia; Handheld; 85mm; f4; 1/60sec

77 (top) Nikon F3; 35mm; Velvia; Handheld; 85mm; f5.6; 1/60sec

77 (bottom) Nikon F3; 35mm; Velvia; Tripod; 180mm; f22; 1sec

78 (top) Nikon F3; 35mm; Velvia; Handheld; 180mm; f5.6; 1/25sec

78 (bottom) Nikon F3; 35mm; Velvia; Handheld; 28mmPC; f8; 1/60sec

79 Nikon F3; 35mm; Velvia; Handheld; 28mmPC; f8; 1/60sec

80 Nikon F3; 35mm; Fuji50D; Handheld; 24mm; f8; 1/30sec

80–1 Nikon F3; 35mm; Kodachrome64; Handheld; 24mm; f8; 1/60sec

82 (top) Nikon F3; 35mm; Fuji50D; Handheld; 35mm; f5.6; 1/25sec

82 (bottom) Nikon F3; 35mm; Kodachrome25; Tripod; 600mm; f5.6; 1/60sec

83 Nikon F3; 35mm; Fuji50D; Handheld; 35mm; f5.6; 1/60sec

84 (top) Nikon F3; 35mm; Velvia; Handheld; 85mm; f5.6; 1/60sec

84 (bottom) Nikon F3; 35mm; Velvia; Handheld; 28mmPC; f8; 1/60sec

85 (top) Nikon F3; 35mm; Kodachrome 64; Tripod; 24mm; f8; 1/15sec; Polariser

85 (bottom) Nikon F3; 35mm; Kodachrome64; Tripod; 300mm; f8; 1/60sec

86 (top) Nikon F3; 35mm; Fuji50D; Handheld; 85mm; f5.6; 1/60sec

86 (bottom) Nikon F3; 35mm; Fuji50D; Handheld; 24mm; f5.6; 1/30sec; Polariser

87 Nikon F3; 35mm; Kodachrome64; Handheld; 35mm; f5.6; 1/60sec

88–9 Nikon F3; 35mm; Fuji50D; Handheld; 85mm; f4; 1/25sec

89 (top) Nikon F3; 35mm; Velvia; Handheld; 35mm; f5.6; 1/60sec; Polariser

89 (bottom) Nikon F3; 35mm; Kodachrome64; Handheld; 35mm; f8; 1/60sec

90–1 Hasselblad 503CX; 6x6; Velvia; Tripod; 80mm; f11; 1/15sec; Polariser

91 Nikon F3; 35mm; Velvia; Handheld; 28mmPC; f8; 1/60sec

THE EAST

92–3 Hasselblad 503CX; 6x6; Velvia; Tripod; 150mm; f22; 1/4sec

94 (top) Nikon F3; 35mm; Velvia; Tripod; 24mm; f8; 1/15sec

94 (bottom) Nikon F3; 35mm; Velvia; Handheld; 28mmPC; f5.6; 1/60sec

94–5 Hasselblad 503CX; 6x6; Velvia; Tripod; 80mm; f22; 2sec

96 (left) Hasselblad 503CX; 6x6; Velvia; Tripod; 50mm; f22; 1/4sec; Polariser

96 (right) Nikon F3; 35mm; Velvia; Handheld; 28mmPC; f8; 1/60sec

97 Hasselblad 503CX; 6x6; Velvia; Tripod; 80mm; f16; 1/8sec; Polariser

98–9 Hasselblad 503CX; 6x6; Velvia; Tripod; 150mm; f11; 1/8sec; Polariser

99 Nikon F3; 35mm; Velvia; Handheld; 28mmPC; f8; 1/60sec

100 Hasselblad 503CX; 6x6; Velvia; Tripod; 150mm; f22; 1/4sec

101 Hasselblad 503CX; 6x6; Velvia; Tripod; 50mm; f22; 1/4sec; Polariser

102 Hasselblad 503CX; 6x6; Velvia; Tripod; 80mm; f16; 1/4sec; Polariser

103 (top) Nikon F3; 35mm; Velvia; Handheld; 28mmPC; f5.6; 1/60sec

103 (bottom) Nikon F3; 35mm; Velvia; Tripod; 180mm; f4; 1/250sec

104 Hasselblad 503CX; 6x6; Velvia; Tripod; 150mm; f8; 1/60sec

105 (top) Nikon F3; 35mm; Velvia; Tripod; 180mm; f16; 1/15sec

105 (bottom) Nikon F3; 35mm; Velvia; Handheld; 85mm; f5.6; 1/125sec

106 Nikon F3; 35mm; Velvia; Handheld; 28mmPC; f8; 1/60sec

107 (top) Nikon F3; 35mm; Velvia; Handheld; 28mmPC; f8; 1/60sec

107 (bottom) Nikon F3; 35mm; Velvia; Handheld; 28mmPC; f8; 1/60sec

THE SOUTH–EAST

108–9 Hasselblad 503CX; 6x6; Velvia; Tripod; 150mm; f22; 1sec

110 Nikon F3; 35mm; Velvia; Handheld; 85mm; f5.6; 1/25sec

110–11 Hasselblad 503CX; 6x6; Velvia; Tripod; 50mm; f8; 1/8sec; Polariser

112 (top) Mamiya 6; 6x6; Velvia; Tripod; 75mm; f22; 1sec

112 (bottom) Nikon F3; 35mm; Velvia; Handheld; 28mmPC; f8; 1/60sec

113 (top) Nikon F3; 35mm; Velvia; Handheld; 85mm; f8; 1/60sec

113 (bottom) Nikon F3; 35mm; Velvia; Handheld; 85mm; f8; 1/60sec

114–15 Nikon F3; 35mm; Velvia; Handheld; 24mm; f4; 1/60sec; Polariser

115 (top) Nikon F3; 35mm; Velvia; Handheld; 28mmPC; f5.6; 1/60sec

115 (bottom) Nikon F3; 35mm; Velvia; Tripod; 85mm; f8; 1/15sec; Polariser

116 Nikon F3; 35mm; Velvia; Handheld; 28mmPC; f8; 1/60sec

117 Nikon F3; 35mm; Velvia; Tripod; 24mm; f4; 1/30sec; Polariser

118 (top) Nikon F3; 35mm; Velvia; Handheld; 28mmPC; f8; 1/60sec

118 (bottom) Hasselblad 503CX; 6x6; Velvia; Tripod; 80mm; f22; 1/2sec; Polariser

119 Nikon F3; 35mm; Velvia; Handheld; 180mm; f4; 1/25sec

120 (left) Nikon F3; 35mm; Velvia; Handheld; 24mm; f8; 1/60sec

120 (right) Nikon F3; 35mm; Velvia; Handheld; 28mmPC; f8; 1/60sec

121 Nikon F3; 35mm; Velvia; Handheld; 28mmPC; f8; 1/60sec

122–3 Hasselblad 503CX; 6x6; Velvia; Tripod; 150mm; f22; 1/4sec

123 Nikon F3; 35mm; Velvia; Tripod; 180mm; f8; 1/60sec

124 (top) Hasselblad 503CX; 6x6; Velvia; Tripod; 150mm; f22; 1/2sec

124 (bottom) Nikon F3; 35mm; Velvia; Handheld; 85mm; f5.6; 1/60sec

125 (top) Nikon F3; 35mm; Velvia; Handheld; 28mmPC; f5.6; 1/60sec

125 (bottom) Nikon F3; 35mm; Velvia; Tripod; 180mm; f16; 1/8sec

126–7 Mamiya 6; 6x6; Velvia; Tripod; 50mm; f22; 1/8sec

126 (bottom) Nikon F3; 35mm; Velvia; Handheld; 85mm; f5.6; 1/25sec

128 Mamiya 6; 6x6; Velvia; Tripod; 50mm; f22; 1/8sec

129 (top) Nikon F3; 35mm; Velvia; Handheld; 28mmPC; f8; 1/60sec

129 (bottom) Nikon F3; 35mm; Velvia; Handheld; 28mmPC; f5.6; 1/60sec

130–1 Mamiya 6; 6x6; Velvia; Tripod; 50mm; f22; 1/2sec

131 (top) Nikon F3; 35mm; Velvia; Tripod; 85mm; f11; 1/30sec

131 (bottom) Nikon F3; 35mm; Velvia; Handheld; 28mmPC; f8; 1/60sec

THE SOUTH–WEST

132–3 Mamiya 6; 6x6; Velvia; Tripod; 75mm; f22; 1/2sec

134–5 Mamiya 6; 6x6; Velvia; Tripod; 50mm; f22; 1/4sec

135 Nikon F3; 35mm; Velvia; Handheld; 24mm; f5.6; 1/60sec

136 (top) Nikon F3; 35mm; Velvia; Handheld; 28mmPC; f5.6; 1/60sec

136 (bottom) Mamiya 6; 6x6; Velvia; Tripod; 50mm; f22; 1/4sec

136–7 Mamiya 6; 6x6; Velvia; Tripod; 50mm; f22; 1/2sec

138–9 Mamiya 6; 6x6; Velvia; Tripod; 50mm; f22; 1/8sec

139 (top) Nikon F3; 35mm; Velvia; Handheld; 85mm; f5.6; 1/60sec

139 (bottom) Nikon F3; 35mm; Velvia; Handheld; 28mmPC; f8; 1/60sec

140 Mamiya 6; 6x6; Velvia; Tripod; 50mm; f22; 8sec

141 (top) Mamiya 6; 6x6; Velvia; Tripod; 75mm; f16; 1/4sec

141 (bottom) Nikon F3; 35mm; Velvia; Tripod; 180mm; f8; 1/15sec

142–3 Mamiya 6; 6x6; Velvia; Tripod; 150mm; f8; 1/30sec

143 (top) Nikon F3; 35mm; Velvia; Handheld; 28mmPC; f8; 1/60sec

143 (bottom) Fuji GX680; 6x8; Velvia; Tripod; 65mm; f22; 8sec

144 (top) Nikon F3; 35mm; Velvia; Handheld; 28mmPC; f5.6; 1/30sec

144 (bottom) Nikon F3; 35mm; Velvia; Tripod; 180mm; f8; 1/60sec

145 (top) Nikon F3; 35mm; Velvia; Handheld; 28mmPC; f8; 1/60sec

145 (bottom) Fuji GX680; 6x8; Velvia; Tripod; 80mm; f32; 1/2sec; Polariser

146–7 Fuji GX680; 6x8; Velvia; Tripod; 300mm; f45; 2sec

146 (bottom) Nikon F3; 35mm; Velvia; Tripod; 180mm; f8; 1/60sec

148 Nikon F3; 35mm; Velvia; Tripod; 24mm; f16; 1/2sec

148–9 Fuji GX680; 6x8; Velvia; Tripod; 300mm; f22; 1sec

150 Mamiya 6; 6x6; Velvia; Tripod; 150mm; f22; 1/4sec

151 Mamiya 6; 6x6; Velvia; Tripod; 50mm; f22; 1/8sec

152 (top) Nikon F3; 35mm; Velvia; Handheld; 180mm; f4; 1/250sec

152 (bottom) Mamiya 6; 6x6; Velvia; Tripod; 50mm; f22; 1/2sec

153 (left) Nikon F3; 35mm; Velvia; Handheld; 35mm; f4; 1/60sec; Polariser

153 (right) Mamiya 6; 6x6; Velvia; Tripod; 50mm; f22; 1/8sec

154 (top) Nikon F3; 35mm; Velvia; Handheld; 35mm; f2.8; 1/60sec; Polariser

154 (bottom) Fuji GX680; 6x8; Velvia; Tripod; 65mm; f32; 1sec

154–5 Fuji GX680; 6x8; Velvia; Tripod; 300mm; f16; 30sec

SELECT BIBLIOGRAPHY

As research for this book spans many years, the bibliography has been restricted mainly to key works and specific references in the text. However, I am indebted to all those authors (often uncredited) who have written or contributed to the countless guide books and leaflets (towns, properties, churches, etc.), which have proved invaluable. The Pevsner-Penguin Buildings of England series have been extremely useful; as have many other county or regional series. Our own books have not been included as there is a full list elsewhere. Ordnance Survey maps, notably the scales 1:25,000 and 1:50,000, deserve a mention as they are so often taken for granted.

ALEXANDER, PETER, (ed.), *William Shakespeare: The Complete Works,* Collins, London, 1951

ATKINSON, JOHN CHRISTOPHER, *Forty Years in a Moorland Parish,* Macmillan, London, 1891

SAVAGE, ANNE, (trans. & coll.), *Anglo-Saxon Chronicle,* Heinemann, London, 1982

AUBREY, JOHN, *Monumenta Britannica* (compiled 1665–93),Dorset Publishing Company, Sherborne, 1980 (1st pub.)

BATES, H.E., *The Pop Larkin Chronicles,* Penguin Books, Harmondsworth, 1991

BEDE, THE VENERABLE, *The Ecclesiastical History of the English Nation,* Dent, London, n.d.

BEDE, THE VENERABLE, *A History of the English Church and People* (trans. Leo Sherley-Price), Penguin Books, Harmondsworth, 1955

CAMDEN, WILLIAM, *Britannia,* Gibson, London, 1695

CAREW, RICHARD, *Survey of Cornwall,* 1602 (new edition, London, 1769)

CARRINGTON, NICHOLAS TOMS, *Dartmoor: A Descriptive Poem,* John Murray, London, 1826

COBBETT, WILLIAM, *Rural Rides,* Penguin Books, Harmondsworth, 1967

COBURN, KATHLEEN, (ed.), *Notebooks of S.T. Coleridge,* Routledge & Kegan Paul, London, 1962–74

DEFOE, DANIEL, *A Tour Thro' the Whole Island of Great Britain* (2 vols.), Davies, London, 1927

DE QUINCEY, THOMAS, *Recollections of the Lakes and the Lake Poets,* Penguin Books, Harmondsworth, 1970

DU MAURIER, DAPHNE, *Enchanted Cornwall,* Michael Joseph, Harmondsworth, 1989

FIELD, WILLIAM, *An Historical and Descriptive Account of the Town and Castle of Warwick and the Neighbouring Spa of Leamington,* Sharpe, 1815

FIENNES, CELIA, (ed. Morris, Christopher), *The Journeys of Celia Fiennes,* Cresset, London, 1947

FRASER, MAXWELL, *Companion into Worcestershire,* Methuen, London, 1939

GULPING, WILLIAM, *Three Essays on Picturesque Beauty; on Picturesque Travel; and on Sketching Landscape,* Blamire, London, 1794

GRIFFIN, A.H., *Inside the Real Lakeland,* Guardian Press, Preston, 1961

HEMMING, PETER, *Windmills in Sussex,* C.W. Daniel, London, 1936

HOEY, GRAHAM, (ed.), *Eastern Gritstone: Stanage* (Peak Rock Climbs – fifth series Vol.1), British Mountaineering Council, Manchester, 1989

HUTCHINSON, THOMAS, (ed.), *The Poetical Works of Wordsworth,* O.U.P., Oxford, 1932

IRELAND, SAMUEL, *Picturesque Views on the Upper, or Warwickshire Avon,* Faulder, 1795

JAMES, HENRY, *English Hours,* Oxford University Press, Oxford, 1981

KIPLING, RUDYARD, *Puck of Pook's Hill,* Macmillan, London, 1937

KIPLING, RUDYARD, *The Works of Rudyard Kipling,* Wordsworth Editions, 1994

KNIGHT, WILLIAM, (ed.), *Journals of Dorothy Wordsworth,* Macmillan, London, 1930

LANGLAND, WILLIAM, *Piers Plowman,* Dent, London, 1912

LANE, MARGARET, *The Tale of Beatrix Potter,* Warne, London, 1968

LELAND, JOHN, (ed. Toulmin Smith, Lucy) *The Itinerary of John Leland* (5 vols.), S. Illinois University, Carbondale, USA, 1964

MARPLES, MORRIS, *White Horses and Other Hill Figures,* Sutton, Stroud, 1981

MAYBERRY, TOM, *Coleridge & Wordsworth in the West Country,* Sutton, Stroud, 1992

MIDMER, ROY, *English Medieval Monasteries 1066–1540,* Heinemann, London, 1979

NAIRN, IAN, AND PEVSNER, NIKOLAUS, *Surrey* (The Buildings of England series), Penguin Books, Harmondsworth, 1962

NICHOLSON, NORMAN, *The Lake District: an Anthology,* Hale, London, 1977

PALMER, WILLIAM T., *The English Lakes,* A. & C. Black, London, 1905

PEVSNER, NIKOLAUS, *Shropshire* (The Buildings of England series), Penguin Books, Harmondsworth, 1958

PEVSNER, NIKOLAUS, *Warwickshire* (The Buildings of England series), Penguin Books, Harmondsworth, 1966

PEVSNER, NIKOLAUS, AND CHERRY, BRIDGET, *Wiltshire,* (The Buildings of England series), Penguin Books, Harmondsworth, 1963

PONTEFRACT, ELLA, *Swaledale,* Dent, London, 1934

PRIESTLEY, J.B., *English Journey,* Heinemann, London, 1934

RUDDER, SAMUEL, *A New History of Gloucestershire,* Rudder, Cirencester, 1779

STEERS, J.A., *The Coastline of England and Wales,* Cambridge University Press, Cambridge, 1969

THORNE, JAMES, *Rambles by Rivers:* The Avon, Knight, 1845

TURNER, W.J., *Exmoor Village,* Harrap, London, 1947

WAINWRIGHT, ALFRED, *A Pictorial Guide to the Lakeland Fells:* Books One to Seven, Westmorland Gazette, 1955–66

WORDSWORTH, DOROTHY, *Illustrated Lakeland Journals,* Collins, London, 1897

WORDSWORTH, WILLIAM, *A Guide through the District of the Lakes in the North of England …* (5th ed.), 1835

WORDSWORTH, WILLIAM, (ed. Darlington, Beth), *Home at Grasmere: Part First, Book First of the Recluse,* Harvester Press, Hassocks, 1977

INDEX